A TIMES BARTHOLOMEW GUIDE
VENICE

First edition prepared by
Claude Janicot

This edition updated by
Didier Sénécal

Our special thanks to
Diego Valeri, for the introductory material

Translation
John Dunmore

Adaptation
Times Editions, Singapore, and Hachette, Paris

Production
Times Editions, Singapore

This edition published in Great Britain by **John Bartholomew & Son Ltd** and **Times Books Ltd,** 16 Golden Square, London W1R 4BN.

This guide is adapted from *À Venise* published by Hachette Guides Bleus, Paris, 1986.

© Hachette Guides Bleus, 1986.
English translation © Hachette Guides Bleus, 1987.
Maps © TCI, Milan 1987; Hachette Guides Bleus, 1987.

British Library Cataloguing in Publication Data

Janicot, Claude
    Venice. — (A Times Bartholomew guide)
    1. Venice (Italy) — Description —
    guide-books
    I. Title   II. Senecal, Didier
    III. À Venise. *English*
    914.5′ 31   DG672
    ISBN 0-7230-0290-8

Printed in Singapore

A TIMES BARTHOLOMEW GUIDE
VENICE

Published by Times Books and
John Bartholomew and Son Ltd

HOW TO USE YOUR GUIDE

Before you leave, look up the information in the section: "Planning Your Trip" (p. 13). On arrival, make use of the addresses and practical information in the section "Amenities in Venice" (p. 43).

The names of the main sites, churches, monuments, museums, hotels, restaurants and shops are followed by a grid reference which will enable you to find their location on the maps (pp. 46-47, 50-51 and 146). Also shown are the numbers of the boat service lines by which they can be reached and the name of the nearest landing-stage.

To find a place, a building or an artist, look up the Index (pp. 154-157).

Telephones: some numbers in Venice are preceded by the area code: 52.

SYMBOLS USED

Sites, monuments, museums, works of art

★ interesting
★ ★ remarkable
★ ★ ★ exceptional

Hotel classification

▲ simple and comfortable
▲ ▲ very comfortable
▲ ▲ ▲ first class hotel
▲ ▲ ▲ ▲ luxury hotel

MAPS

Location map, **12**
Access roads to Venice (I), **15**
Overall view, with Murano (II), **46-47**
Center of Venice (III), **50-51**
The Lido (IV), **146**

▬ CONTENTS

Photo credits: Atelier Le Roseau, pp. 103, 131. – C. Boisvieux, pp. 39, 87, 107, 110, 135, 143. – B. Millé, p. 23. – P. Milleron, pp. 78, 79, 86, 95, 114, 115, 123, 139. – P. de Panthou, pp. 6, 11, 26, 31, 42, 74, 82, 91, 99.

INTRODUCTION TO VENICE

Back in May 1544 the poet Aretino wrote a letter to his friend, Titian, describing the beauty of the Venetian sky which he beheld framed in a high window of his house on the Rialto. He had felt ill and depressed, with a lingering sense of despair, when he raised his eyes heavenwards and found himself not merely consoled but uplifted by the sight of this "aery light", this "lovely picture of light and shade". The last traces of his fever and all his cares fell away, leaving him in a state of ecstasy.

"Those buildings, above all," he wrote, "which are indeed built of stone, seemed to be carved from the very stuff of which dreams are made. And the light, so pure and clear in places, dreary in others — imagine how astonished I was by the clouds in all their different tones! Those closest glowed and blazed; those further off took on hues of soft crimson.

"How beautiful it was to see Nature's brush drawing the light towards the background of the picture beyond the *palazzi*, just as Titian himself had done when painting such scenes! Here a glimpse of green tinged with blue, (over) yonder a greenish blue, colors mixed by Nature, that master of masters. Her touches of light and dark (tones) gave depth or relief to what she wanted to push into the background or to bring forward, so much so that I called out three or four times: 'Oh, Titian, where are you now?' ..."

To explore the waterways of Venice is to lose oneself in a ceaseless interplay of colors and reflections.

No one has ever written with such precision and accuracy about Venice, nor described so well the striking diversity of this city conjured out of the waters by some magician of light.

The very essence of Venice, home of beauty and of poetry, seems indeed to reside more in the quality of the light, and the atmosphere, than in its magnificent architecture. Before Venice existed, that same light played over the waters, calling it forth, waiting for the moment when it could begin its endless variations of tones and shadows, transforming the city and altering perspectives. This quality is at the heart of Venice's uniqueness.

Venice is a city of infinite variety. It is never the same. It never stands still, because the light never ceases to create and to recreate it anew. The explanation is that this light is not of the earth, but of the water — water which never sleeps, constantly mirroring and multiplying the innumerable variations of the Venetian sky.

Thus, caught between two mirrors — one which reflects the sky, the other the water — Venice stands in an elusive interplay of daylight and darkness, reborn afresh with each dawn.

The wind plays its part as well, rippling the waters and driving clouds which darken the city only to part again and let the sun pour down. The mere breath of the *garbino* or the *libeccio* will change the hues of Venice, set off a new vibration, a new luminescence across the Sea of Venice — that interior sea they call the lagoon. A small cloud passing over the face of the sun will tarnish the splendor of sea and sky; colors which a moment earlier sparkled like jewels are dulled; buildings which had called out for our attention become veiled and recede into the half-light.

The wind drops and its absence again transforms the city. The lagoon now turns into a vast sheet of gray steel or a pavement of lapis-lazuli. Overhead, the sky stretches out like a pale blue canopy flecked with silver. Then there is the fog. Lagoon and buildings dissolve into it, the canals are suddenly choked with gray vapor. With the rain, Venice is imprisoned in a cage of shining, singing threads. Finally, there are the moons, two moons shedding their enchantment across Venice — one above, one reflected in the water, scattering beams of pale or reddish gold.

There lies Venice's particular charm. No one can penetrate that light without feeling that he has somehow left the ordinary world and is now "elsewhere". It is a place where the laws of space and time are different, where what is normally stable and firmly rooted in the earth wavers and ripples, where rationality ends and each certainty dissolves into one of a range of possibilities. The frontiers of past and present, of waking and dreaming, lose their reality. It is this aura of magic which Aretino, one evening in May 1544, described so subtly and with such perceptiveness.

Fifteen centuries ago, when Ravenna was slumbering in the shade of its forest, somberly resplendent like a rich basilica, nothing here foreshadowed the birth of Venice. There was only a great marsh edged with a sandy wasteland which was overgrown with reeds and dotted with small, aggressively green islands which were invaded and ravaged from time to time by angry torrents of river and sea. A few hardy fisherfolk eked out an existence along the shore or on some of the islands; there were a few salt gatherers and market gardeners and a handful of mariners, with a loose allegiance to distant Rome and later to Byzantium, and with no other history than the daily routine of their struggle for survival. The tide rose daily, as it still does to this day, covering the lowest lying areas and ceaselessly eroding the few patches of land on which they desperately clung to life.

Venice, today, is only a city which, like others, is compelled to accept the trials as well as the advantages of modern life, but no one would dare claim that it is a town like any other. Today, even more than in the past, Venice represents a unique version of what a community can be.

It is the only city in the world built entirely on water, the only one created by man for the purpose of living as a community on water. Rather than a city of industrious beavers, it is more like an enormous ship, firmly anchored, where a nation of sailors spend their days in harmony — when they are not away on adventurous voyages. What strikes the outsider even more than the appearance of this city, is how the people of Venice have, time and again, transformed necessity into freedom, the constraints of their environment into a source of moral energy and the very desolation of the lagoon into a rare beauty. Even more striking is the development of a distinct culture which has survived largely untouched through the vicissitudes of a thousand years. Venice is the product of faith and of willpower. It is a poem in stone and survives as a poem in its original form and spirit although its historical significance has now faded away, never to return.

Venice not only survives, it is recreated anew each morning as if the primeval energy that first drew it out of the waters is still as strong as it ever was. The environment which gave it birth is still there: the lagoon and the waters that move through its canals as through so many veins, the slender shoreline that defends it from the restless sea, the small cultivated islands and the deserted ones. The shimmering waters still reflect the sky, spreading that all-embracing light over the glinting waves.

Set in this frame, the city watches over the vast wealth of art treasures the centuries have bestowed. An ancient faith still glows in the churches behind the sensual ostentation of the mosaics and the paintings. The *palazzi*, with their profusion of windows, balconies and loggias, remind us that open trust and the friendship of neighbors were essential features of city life. The houses soar from the shadows of the *calli* towards the sun and the salty sea air. The bridges arch gracefully over the canal to soften the geometrical patterns of the squares and the alleyways. Greenery and summer flowers cascade over walls towards the waters of a quiet canal, a hint of Venice's tiny secret gardens...

Time, so quick to cheapen and destroy what is only material, has been powerless or, at any rate, respectful towards this poetry. We have to accept that in centuries to come, Venice the survivor will die, as everything that lives must do but we can be confident that in that distant future, its ghost will still haunt the waters that witnessed its birth. There will always be, in this special corner of the world,

St Mark's Square remains the heart of the city: filled with life and excitement, sundrenched by day, startlingly beautiful by night.

that unique interplay of light and lagoon, that infinite range of hues and shades and, with every dawn, there will arise out of the fleeing darkness a new Venice, fashioned from light, water and memories. It will not, after all, be so very different from the one we can see today which, to use the words of Dante, is a "true substance" that looks like the "reflection of an image".

Diego Valeri

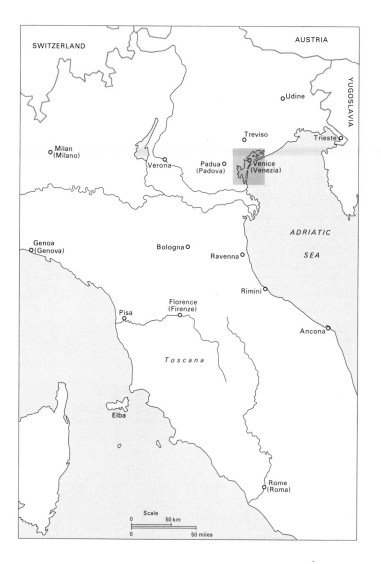

PLANNING YOUR TRIP

This chapter contains all the information you require before you leave: climate, formalities, currency, means of travel, useful addresses.

▬ *WHEN TO VISIT VENICE?*

If you can choose, go in spring or, better still, in autumn before October because the fascinating play of light is at its best then. Broadly speaking, it is coldest in January, and the wettest month is October. Visitors will find the heat of the summer more bearable in July than in August. At this time of year, the crowds thronging the *calli* disrupt Venice's peaceful and quiet atmosphere and it is advisable to choose hotels and restaurants with air-conditioning.

Your choice need not be determined by the seasons or by the dates when you normally go on vacation. A festival or a cultural event may attract you, and most of them are held in the summer. The following information may assist you.

If you like music: symphony concerts are held at *La Fenice* from May to July and from September to December. Chamber music concerts are held from March to June; jazz concerts and the *Festival of Contemporary Music* take place in September. *La Fenice* also presents opera from December to May. Bookings: at the theater from 10 am – 12 noon and from 5 pm – 7 pm; you can also reserve for the *Malibran Theater* which shares *La Fenice's* program. Excellent concerts are given under the auspices of the artistic circle and of the *Cini Foundation* at San Giorgio Maggiore.

If you like drama and plays: the time to go to Venice is September to October for the *Festival of Prose Drama* at the *Teatro del Ridotto*. Like the *Malibran* and the *Goldoni*, it presents a number of excellent plays from January to May and from October to December. Occasional performances are also presented in the open-air theater of the *Cini Foundation*.

If you like modern art: go during the summer, from June to September (on even-numbered years only), for the *Biennale* in the *Giardini* pavilions.

If you enjoy bargain hunting: antique and second-hand dealers from all over Italy congregate in the *Campo San*

Maurizio four times a year: in Holy Week from Thursday to Saturday, during the Ascension long weekend; on the third Friday, Saturday and Sunday of September (during the Feast of St Maurice) and on the Friday, Saturday and Sunday before Christmas. Of course, you can bargain over prices — and indeed you should.

If you are a follower of the seventh art: you will rush to the Lido in August-September for the *Mostra d'Arte Cinematografica* (film festival) held at the Palace of the Cinema.

If you like traditional festivals: you can choose May for the Ascension, the *Festa della Sensa*; July (3rd Sunday) for the *Festa del Redentore* (see p. 109 and p. 140) which ends with a truly extraordinary fireworks display; or September (1st Sunday) for the great regatta (*Regata Storica*), the most spectacular of Venetian festivals. Do not overlook the feasts celebrating the *Madonna della Salute* (November 21), the Purification of the Virgin at *Santa Maria Formosa* (February 2), and St Mark (April 25).

The Carnival

There is a time of year when Venice gives free rein to every passion and every excess, when ancient rites prevail. This is in February or early March (depending on the date of Mardi Gras) when a "fever" comes over everyone. The Carnival brings out the masks, the burlesque or macabre sarabands, the balls and the pageants. For some years now, these events have attracted thousands of people from every corner of the world. It is then impossible to find a room or even a seat on a train. You are therefore advised to reserve your room at least two months ahead.

Average Temperatures (low and high for each month)

	January		February		March	
Fahrenheit	32.9	43.2	34.5	45.8	40.8	54.1
Celsius	0.5	6.2	1.4	7.7	4.9	12.3
	April		May		June	
Fahrenheit	49.3	63.1	57	70.7	63.7	77.5
Celsius	9.6	17.3	13.9	21.5	17.6	25.3
	July		August		September	
Fahrenheit	67.3	82.2	66.7	82	61.9	77.9
Celsius	19.6	27.9	19.3	27.8	16.6	25.5
	October		November		December	
Fahrenheit	52	65	43	54.1	36.5	45.8
Celsius	11.1	18.3	6.1	12.3	2.5	7.7

▬ FORMALITIES

Visas are not required for U.S., Canada, U.K. and most Commonwealth nationals. However, a valid passport is required. It is advisable to check with your travel agent or an Italian consulate prior to your departure. Cars may be taken into Italy on presentation of a valid driving license (preferably an international driving license) and the international green

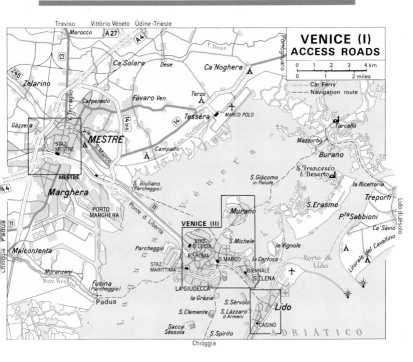

insurance card which your insurance company will supply on request.

Pets in Venice

Cats and dogs are allowed into Italy on production of a health certificate and an anti-rabies vaccination certificate. Italian law requires dogs to be muzzled in public areas and on public transport, and owners are required to clean any droppings without delay. Animals are not allowed in museums or in public gardens, and a number of hotels and restaurants do not admit them. You would be well advised to obtain further information before you start showing the City of the Doges to your pet companion...

▬ MONEY MATTERS

Currency and Foreign Exchange

The unit of currency is the *lira* (plural *lire*). Coins are available in denominations of 50, 100, 200, 500 lire, and banknotes in 500, 1000, 2000, 5000, 10,000, 20,000, 50,000 and 100,000 lire. Inquire from your bank about exchange control regulations, which change from time to time, and for the latest exchange rate for the *lira* on the international market. If you pay for purchases in Italy by means of a credit card, these transactions are not affected by foreign exchange regulations. Note that the importation of currency is limited to 200,000 lire per person. When buying travellers cheques, ensure that the issuing bank is affiliated with an Italian bank. This will avoid long delays at a foreign exchange counter.

Budgeting

When making up your budget, remember that Venice is the most expensive city in Italy. If you have not booked on an all-inclusive basis, allow between 178,000 and 200,000 lire per day for two people. This would cover hotels and restaurant meals, as well as pocket money for refreshments and admission to museums and art galleries.

▬ HOW TO GET THERE

By Air and by Water

An ideal and logical way of going to Venice would be to approach the city by sea, but this is only possible if you are coming from Greece, Yugoslavia or the eastern Mediterranean.

Even though arriving by sea presents a picture any visitor would treasure, Venice still offers the visitor a rare surprise if coming by air or even by train.

The *Marco Polo* airport is on the mainland by the lagoon, so that when you leave the terminal you can choose between a bus and a motor boat. The bus will take you in 30 minutes to the *Piazzale Roma* (Map II C-1) — where you would also arrive if you came by car. The *motoscafo* (motorboat) will take you, also in 30 minutes, to the San Marco landing stage (Map III F-4) beside the *Giardinetti Reali*. Taking the motorboat is much more enjoyable than the bus: after seeing the full sweep of the sublime city from the sky, you will now discover it little by little, like a navigator coming from a far-away land; you will see it even better than if you approached from the sea, because you will pass in front of the islands of Murano and San Michele and be able to admire the silhouette of Venice against the sunlit sky as you come in from the north. Then, at the halfway mark, your boat rounds the island of Sant' Elena and, passing along the lagoon side of the Lido, it enters the San Marco basin to reach the landing stage. In this way, before you set foot on dry land, you will have discovered the Palace of the Doges, the Campanile and the island of San Giorgio Maggiore.

By Train

If you go by train, you will still find the approach to Venice fascinating but don't look out of the window after leaving Mestre railway station: between Mestre and the Venice station, the train slowly crosses the Liberty Bridge, wending its way over 2½ miles/4 km of lagoon with a background of industrial and petrochemical works and not a glimpse of the real Venice — read your paper or a detective novel! When you leave the station in Venice, which is just like any other railway station, you will find yourself walking down wide steps, as though you were coming out of a palace or a church, and you will be plunged immediately into a true Venetian scene at the edge of the Grand Canal. To your left, at *S. Lucia* landing stage (Map II B-1), the *motoscafi* of Line 2 wait to take you to the center together with your luggage by way of the *Rio Nuovo* and the Grand Canal, all in less than a quarter of an hour.

The Return of the Orient Express
For a century the Orient Express was synonymous with luxury train travel. Steaming through Europe, it was a romantic symbol which soon became the favorite means of transport among rich and important people — politicians, Russian princes, actresses, spies... Today, meticulously restored, the Venice-Simplon Orient Express has brought back the splendor of olden times, with its refined decor, wood paneling, plush seats and Lalique glass. To find out about the Orient Express, contact:
Sea Containers House, 20 Upper Ground, London SE.1, tel. (01) 928-5837; telex: 895-58-03.
Suite 1235, One World Trade Center, New York, NY 10048, tel. (212) 938-6830 or (800) 524-2420; telex: WUD645446.

For Car Drivers
The *Pachetto Italia*, a book of petrol coupons, allows you to save on the cost of petrol, and also gives you reduced rates on Italian motorway toll charges as well as access to a free emergency repair service provided by the A.C.I. (Automobile Club of Italy) centers. On the road, phone 116; on the motorway, use the S.O.S. stands. The *Pachetto Italia* is on sale outside Italy in a number of banks, including the Banco di Roma, and in offices of the A.C.I. You can pay for them in any currency except Italian.

Driving to Venice, you will follow the motorway for practically the entire journey but as soon as you have to leave the motorway and cross the lagoon, you will encounter difficulties. The large parking area of the *Piazzale Roma* (Map II C-1) is usually full up and open-air parking facilities on the artificial island of *Tronchetto* are seldom any better (follow the light panels which, as you leave Mestre, indicate available parking spaces). If you can't find a place for your car, you may decide to take it on the *nave traghetto*, the car ferry, and leave it at the *Lido* (at your own risk, because there are no supervised car parks there). This unforgettable short cruise will enable you to discover the city from the lagoon, as your boat passes Venice between the Palace of the Doges and the island of S. Giorgio Maggiore.

The *motoscafi* take only 10 minutes to reach the historic old city center (*S. Zaccaria* landing stage, Map III B-6) from the Lido.

Book in Advance
Although generally expensive, hotels in Venice are busy for much of the year and you are strongly urged to make reservations several weeks ahead. It is often wise to pay for an all-inclusive tour, plane or train and hotel (bed and breakfast). There are also a number of different package tours and visits that enable you to see the maximum possible in the shortest time. Ask at your travel agency.

▬ *BEFORE YOU LEAVE: SOME USEFUL ADDRESSES*

The larger cities of the English-speaking world have an Italian consulate or a consular agent; some have a branch of the Italian State Tourist Office (E.N.I.T.) or of the airline, Alitalia, which often acts as E.N.I.T.'s representative and can provide you with information about traveling to Italy. Most travel agencies and airlines should also be able to give you details on current requirements (valid passport, visa if applicable, etc.). The C.I.T. is the Italian Tourist Co., the official representative of the Italian railways and one of Italy's most important tourist organizations.

Australia
Embassy:
Canberra, 12 Grey St., Deakin ACT 2000, tel. (6) 733-333
Consulates:
Adelaide, 186 Grenhill Rd., Parkside SA 5063, tel. (8) 272-0344
Brisbane, 158 Moray St., New Farm QLD 4005, tel. (7) 358-4344
Melbourne, 34 Anderson St., South Yarra VIC 3141, tel. (3) 267-5744
Perth, 31 Labouchere Rd., South Perth, WA 6151, tel. (9) 367-8922
Sydney, 100 William St., NSW 2000, tel. (2) 358-2955
E.N.I.T.:
Sydney, c/o Alitalia, AGC House, 124 Philip St., NSW 2009, tel. (2) 221-3620
C.I.T.:
Melbourne, 500 Collins St., VIC 3000, tel. (3) 612-774
Sydney, 123 Clarence St., NSW 2000, tel. (2) 294-754

Canada
Embassy:
Ottawa, 275 Slater St., tel. (613) 232-2401
Consulates:
Montreal, 3489 Drummond St., tel. (514) 849-8351
Toronto, 136 Beverly St., tel. (416) 977-1566
Vancouver, Suite 505-1200 Burrard St., tel. (604) 684-7288
E.N.I.T.:
Montreal, Montreal Store 56, Plaza 3, Place Ville-Marie, tel. (514) 866-7667
C.I.T.:
Toronto, 13 Balmuto St., tel. (416) 927-7712

Great Britain
Embassy:
London, 14 Three Kings Yard, Davies St., W1Y 2EH, tel. 629-8200
Consulates:
London, Heathcote House, 20 Savile Row, W1X 2DQ, tel. 235-9371
Edinburgh, 2 Melville Crescent, EH3 7JA, tel. 226-3631
Manchester, St James' Building, 79 Oxford St., tel. 236-9024
E.N.I.T.:
London, 200 Regent St., W.1, tel. 734-4631; 1 Princess St., W1R 8AY, tel. 408-1254
C.I.T.:
London, 50/51 Conduit St., London W1R 9FB, tel. 434-3844

Hong Kong
Consulates:
801 Hutchison House, 10 Harcourt Rd., tel. (5) 220-033

E.N.I.T.:
c/o Alitalia, Hilton Hotel, Queen's Road Central, (P.O.Box 1514) tel. (5) 237-041

Ireland
Embassy:
Dublin, 12 Fitzwilliam Square, Dublin 2, tel. (353) 760-366
Consulates:
Belfast, 2 Kincraig Park, Newtownabbey, BT36 7QA, tel. (232) 778-353

New Zealand
Embassy:
Wellington, 34 Grant Rd., tel. (4) 736-667
E.N.I.T.:
Auckland, c/o Alitalia, 95 Queen St., tel. (9) 794-455

South Africa
Embassy:
Pretoria, 796 Georgelaan Avenue, Arcadia 0083, tel. 435-451
E.N.I.T.:
Johannesburg, London House, 21 Loveday St., Johannesburg 2000 (P.O.Box 6507), tel. 838-3247

United States
Consulates:
Boston, 101 Tremont St., MA 02108, tel. (617) 542-0483
Los Angeles, 11661 San Vicente Boulevard, Suite 911, CA 90049, tel. (213) 826-5998
New York, 690 Park Avenue, NY 10021, tel. (212) 737-9100
San Francisco, 2590 Webster St., CA 94115, tel. (415) 931-4924
E.N.I.T.:
New York, 630 Fifth Avenue, NY 10111, tel. (212) 245-4961
Chicago, 500 N. Michigan Avenue, Ill 60611, tel. (312) 644-0990
San Francisco, 360 Post St., CA 94108, tel. (415) 392-6206
C.I.T.:
Los Angeles, Suite 819, 15760 Ventura Boulevard, CA 91436, tel. (213) 783-7245
New York, 666 Fifth Avenue, NY 10103, tel. (212) 397-9300

VENICE IN HISTORY

First and foremost, Venice is an adventure – that of a community of merchants who played a major role in the history of relations between Europe and the East, while struggling heroically against the elements, particularly the sea.

The Venetians were island people, protected from the Barbarians of the mainland by a small lagoon which they used, with the help of immense architectural works, to preserve their isolation and defend their independence. They halted the advance of the mud and the silt by taming the rivers – even diverting the River Brenta – and they dredged channels to control the ebb and flow of the tide into the lagoon.

This "republic of beavers", as Goethe called them, displayed a tenacity more frequently credited to those other lowland dwellers, the Dutch. The same determination earned them a place in the history of international trade somewhere between the Phoenicians of Antiquity and the English traders of more recent times. Like the Phoenicians, they monopolized Mediterranean trade; like the English they built a fleet the rest of the world had to contend with. Later, when America was discovered and the route to India was opened, the center of gravity of trade and politics shifted away.

PROSPERITY BORN OUT OF A CRUSADE

Venice attained greatness through its ships, not merely because of the cargo they carried, but also because, like the Phoenicians, they transported the troops of their temporary allies and friends to distant theaters of war.

The Venetians – more correctly, the Veneti – were originally land-dwellers occupying an area between the Po valley, the Alps and the Adriatic. They sought refuge on the offshore islands to escape Attila the Hun and eventually, under pressure from the Lombards, abandoned the mainland altogether. At first, they settled along the sandspits of *Malamocco* and *Iesolo*, and islets such as *Torcello*, but gradually concentrated their community on the larger archipelago, the *Rialto*, which offered the advantage of a deeper channel. They ensured their survival, and in time asserted their independence, by making themselves indispensable to the Byzantine empire which had need of their ships.

When the power of Byzantium declined, the Venetians turned to the Crusaders, using the same tactics by which they had achieved their autonomy. Their ships carried the armies of the Fourth Crusade, but the elderly Venetian Doge, *Enrico Dandolo*, persuaded the Crusade to postpone its primary objective, in favor of going to Constantinople which was known to be in a state of weakness. Thus, when the fabled city fell, Venice's men marched in by the side of the Crusaders and proudly brought back the Crusaders' war booty, including the four famous brass horses of San Marco.

MARCO POLO: A MODEL MERCHANT

The Venetians were now in control of all trade between East and West. Masters of the Mediterranean lines of communication, they transformed their port into a market for the entire European hinterland. In addition, they were able to use their commercial outposts in Egypt and Asia Minor to establish themselves as sole intermediaries between Europe, India and China.

It was around this time that Marco Polo began his amazing travels. His talent as a diplomat and his commercial initiatives have earned him a well-deserved place among the major figures of Venetian history. This was in the 13th century: Venetian merchants were traveling the silk and spice routes of central and eastern Asia. When they sensed that they had exhausted a district's commercial potential, the traders moved on, but instead of going home they had the foresight and the daring to reinvest their profits in yet another area and, when they finally returned to Venice with the fortune they had accumulated, they increased it even further by financing new trading voyages.

THE WORLD'S FIRST BANKERS

While Europe was still struggling in medieval darkness, the Venetians were refining their trading methods still further, with initiatives that were remarkably advanced for their time. The merchants of the Rialto sent agents to their various overseas bases and built up a trading network. As a result, the Stock Exchange, banking, book keeping and bills of exchange all originated in Venice.

Forewarned by their agents of fluctuations in the prices of goods and raw materials, they were able to determine with precision what the prices should be on the Rialto. Again, by using their overseas agents, they sent out letters, keeping duplicate copies, which became in effect commercial contracts. They could now eliminate uncertainty and consequently the risks they took by reducing the need to move gold or funds, since payments could be made by bills of exchange drawn between the head office and its branches. This is why they became the first merchants in the Western world to keep sophisticated account books instead of merely recording receipts and expenses. They could consequently assess at any time how well their business was doing and analyze its overall or local operations.

This remarkable organization, which was quite unlike anything Westerners were so far accustomed to, provides the key to an understanding of Venice's disproportionate importance in European commerce. Eastern and northern European trade passed through Venice and later, when Venice had defeated Genoa after a struggle which lasted throughout the 14th century, extended to the western Mediterranean. Reaching the peak of its commercial supremacy, Venice established its domination over parts of the mainland from which the early Veneti had come — *Padua, Vicenza, Brescia, Verona* and even *Bergamo*.

This growth led the Venetians to develop a particular form of government appropriate to a nation of powerful merchants.

AN UNUSUAL REPUBLIC

For the first few centuries of their settlement, the inhabitants of the Lagoon were governed by "Tribuni Maritimi" (Maritime Tribunes) who, in the main, were aristocrats from Ravenna nominated by the Emperor's representative in the region. Later, under the Byzantine Empire, the administrative functions were carried out by an official appointed by the Central Government, who, in time, was replaced by a single governor known as the. Doge (from the Latin *dux*, leader) elected by the people. At the end of the 12th century, when Venice finally

Palace of the Doges: the Tetrarchs. This is an Egyptian or Syrian work of the 4th century in porphyry which, so legend tells us, represents four Saracens turned to stone for having attempted to steal the treasure of San Marco.

became independent, the great families began by degrees to assume the right of electing the Doge. Representatives of these families met as an assembly of elders, calling themselves the "Great Council" (founded in 1143). In this way, the republic became aristocratic.

In 1297 the "Serrata" decree (literally, "the Locking") finally established that membership of the Great Council would henceforth be a hereditary privilege, limited to a closed caste of families whose names were inscribed in the famous "Libro d'Oro" (Golden Book).

When Venice reached the zenith of its prosperity at the end of the 13th century, various new institutions began to emerge. The Great Council developed smaller, more specialized bodies, such as the Lesser Council (executive), the Council of Forty or "Quarantia" (judiciary) and the Senate (responsible for general policy). The Great Council was also responsible for the selection of the growing number of officials needed to administer the City and Empire. The Doge himself, elected for life, was inevitably open to the temptation of monopolizing power, and, to avert this eventuality, the dreaded Council of Ten was created. The Council of Ten was essentially a secret police organization, and so great was its influence that it did not hesitate to execute the Doge Marino Faliero on a charge of treason.

It was really an oligarchy which opened the door to every kind of political intrigue. Nonetheless, the republic of Venice was an exceptionally advanced concept for the times. The very structure of the city, where noblemen's houses stood side by side with the homes of artisans, confirmed it. It was the only city-state of the Middle Ages and Renaissance to avoid a social revolution.

FROM ART COLLECTORS TO ART PATRONS

Through the spoils of war, and then through trading in works of art, Venice's *nouveaux riches* had accumulated such wonders in their city that their descendants became accustomed to regarding the treasures among which they lived as essential features of the good life. When Venice's maritime power began to wane towards the end of the 15th century, an inbred taste for fine architecture, sculpture, painting, literature and music gave rise both to vocations and to patronage of the arts.

Beginning in the 15th century, solidly entrenched in their city and protected by buffer zones, the Venetians turned to painting. The Venetian school, with its distinctive use of color, was founded by the *Bellini* family whose most famous son, *Giovanni*, created peerless Madonnas. This school would later produce such masters as *Giorgione*, *Titian*, *Veronese* and *Tintoretto*.

Others, however, uninfluenced by this school, became equally famous, among them *Lotto* and *Carpaccio*.

VASCO DA GAMA AND THE DECLINE OF VENICE

Venetian painting emerged when the city was reaching the pinnacle of its power and it developed during the Renaissance, a difficult period for the "most serene" republic. Constantinople had fallen to the Ottomans but, worse still, Vasco da Gama, a Portuguese explorer, had made his name famous through the discovery of the route to India. Venice, however, was powerful, rich and intelligent enough to cling to its rank until the end of the 18th century. Driven from the eastern Mediterranean, Venice held the Turks in check at the sea battle of *Lepanto* (1571). Thus Venice preserved its freedom but it could not prevent them from threatening the Adriatic by sending their troops across land. There were still the Papal States as well as Spain to contend with until, eventually, the proud republic fell to the armies of Napoleon. He used the city as an item of barter and handed it to Austria. It took a plebiscite in 1866 for Venice finally to become a part of Italy.

A PLACE IN THE MODERN WORLD

Venice has sought, with success, to remain true to its genius and its past by promoting international cultural and artistic exchanges, thanks to university foundations, the *Modern Art Bienniale* and the *International Film Festival*. It has even managed to rebuild and preserve its sea trade – Venice is Italy's second largest port – mostly with Mediterranean and Black Sea ports. The city remains one of central Europe's main outlets.

Venice has thus retained its traditions and influence, in spite of implacable, ongoing decline. During the sunset years of the 18th century, Venice contributed painters of genius to the world: *Tiepolo*, famous for his painted ceilings, *Guardi* and *Canaletto*, masters of the descriptive and anecdotal styles, testimony of Venetian contemporary life. Home of the chapelmaster *Antonio Vivaldi*, Venice was, and remains, a major world center for classical and modern music, opera (*La Traviata* and *Rigoletto* were first produced at *La Fenice*) and theater.

Venice's immense cultural heritage means that saving the city is no parochial concern. It concerns more than Italy – Europe and the Americas are involved. UNESCO, as well as Italian, U.S., French, British and German organizations are cooperating to save and restore endangered buildings and works of art.

ART IN VENICE

Venice or Florence? A great many famous writers and millions of ordinary visitors have compared Venice with Florence, contrasting their particular appeal and assessing their importance in the history of art. Venice, it is true, was not a leader in the great movement known as the Renaissance, joining in relatively late. It is also true to say that it cannot lay claim to such world famous figures as Florence's Leonardo da Vinci or Michelangelo. But if Florence had no rival in the 15th century, Venice triumphs in the regularity with which art treasures were acquired. From the Byzantine period to Neo-Classicism, by way of the Romanesque, the Gothic, the Renaissance and the Baroque periods, Venice never ceased to produce great buildings, mosaics, sculptures and paintings, and its great strength is in having succeeded so well in merging them into a harmonious whole.

ARCHITECTURE

Not surprisingly for a city which turned in its earliest years towards the Orient, Venice was strongly influenced by Byzantium. We see it in the great cathedral of Torcello, built in the 7th century and rebuilt in the 11th, as well as in the basilica of San Marco, reminiscent in many ways of Constantinople's Saint Sophia. This Oriental touch combined with Romanesque art to form an original style exemplified by the church of SS. Maria e Donato at Murano; later, Gothic art would incorporate the Moorish elements.

Detail of the mosaic covering the narthex of the basilica of S. Marco, seemingly inspired by old illuminated manuscripts.

Gothic art was particularly well adapted to the lake-like setting and to the strong Venetian light. The slenderness of the Gothic pillars was especially welcome in view of the silty soil on which the foundations had to rest. The need for buildings to be light-weight explains why most churches have ceilings made of timber rather than stone vaults. The main examples of this style are the Palace of the Doges, the Frari and SS. Giovanni e Paolo. It is echoed in the noblemen's residences: the *palazzi* of the Grand Canal display no element of defensiveness but, instead, they are symbols of their owners' social success; bricks were normally used, except for the facades, which were adorned with marble loggias and porticos.

During the 15th century, while the Renaissance was at its peak in Florence, the flamboyant Gothic style was flourishing – the best example is the Ca' d'Oro – but the new architecture was on its way from Lombardy, with Pietro Lombardo (*c.* 1435–1515) and his sons, Tullio and Antonio. Among their achievements are the church of Santa Maria dei Miracoli and the Scuola Grande di San Marco. In the same line, we have Sansovino (Jacopo Tatti, 1486-1570), famous for the *logetta* of the San Marco campanile, and Andrea Palladio (1508-1580), a theorist and advocate of symmetry and functionalism notable for his graceful designs of facades and his use of classical motifs. Several churches in Venice are by Palladio, including the San Giorgio Maggiore and Il Redentore on the island of Giudecca, as well as a number of private villas along the shores of the Brenta and in and around Vicenza. The "Palladian" style greatly influenced English architects such as Inigo Jones and Christopher Wren.

The 17th century saw the triumph of the Baroque style with the highly productive architect Baldassare Longhena (1598-1682) to whom we owe the churches of Santa Maria della Salute and the Scalzi, as well as the Pesaro and Rezzonico palaces. Later, new buildings tended to be designed so as to harmonize with earlier ones: with a few exceptions, pastiche replaced originality.

SCULPTURE

After the great sculptors of the Venetian Gothic period, Giovanni and Bartolomeo Bon (see the *Porta della Calla* in the Palace of the Doges), the Lombardo family followed (tombs of the Doges, Franchetti Gallery). From Florence came Andrea Verrocchio (1435-1488) whose equestrian statue of the *condottiere* Colleoni is one of the greatest of its genre (Campo SS. Giovanni e Paolo, Map III B-C-6) in the world. After Sansovino, whose talents as a sculptor matched his skills as an architect (Museo

Correr), and Alessandro Vittoria (Museo Correr, stuccos in the Libreria Vecchia, Palace of the Doges) came Antonio Canova (1757-1822), the greatest sculptor of the Neo-Classical period (Museo Correr).

THE GREAT VENETIAN PAINTERS

Venice's earliest artists were the Greek mosaicists who were called upon to decorate the basilica of San Marco. The art of the mosaic worker, which survived into the 19th century, soon had to take second place to painting: in the middle of the 14th century, Paolo Veneziano (Accademia, Frari, etc.) developed a refined style which, although still strongly influenced by Byzantine traditions, opened the way to the outstanding Venetian school.

From Bellini to the masters of the 18th century, a succession of famous painters raised the use of color to new heights. As their works represent an essential part of Venice's appeal, we provide below a brief biographical note in chronological order for each of them, and the main museums, palaces and churches where their paintings may be viewed (refer to the Index to find the appropriate itinerary).

Bellini, Jacopo (*c.* 1400-1470)
Less gifted than his two sons, Jacopo Bellini played a major role in the history of Venetian painting, gradually freeing himself from Gothic influences to spend his later years in the study of perspective and composition. It was through him that the spirit of the Renaissance reached Venice.
For his works, visit: Accademia, Museo Correr.

Bellini, Gentile (*c.* 1429-1507)
A pupil of his father, he was also influenced by his brother, Giovanni, with whom he collaborated, and by Mantegna. His talent for portraiture resulted in his being named official portraitist to the Republic (portraits of Doges, of Sultan Muhammed II, *et al*). The first painter to depict daily life in the city in large-scale narrative paintings, he was the precursor of a pictorial style which had considerable appeal until the 18th century.
For his works, visit: Accademia, Museo Correr.

Bellini, Giovanni or Giambellino (*c.* 1430-1516)
"His most characteristic feature," wrote Diego Valeri, "is the revelation of a new atmosphere, which is Venice's special light. What gives him so much power, in spite of his spirit of lyricism, is his gift of expressing in paint that quivering, warm, moist luminosity which surrounds the reality of Venice like golden pollen. Giovanni Bellini

opened up the rich lode of Venetian painting, leading the way to modern art."

He can be regarded as the founding father of the Venetian school, who combined the innovations of his father and of his brother-in-law, Mantegna, with Florentine forms and Flemish techniques. His varied output includes small allegorical paintings as well as *pietàs* and large compositions showing saints surrounding the Virgin Mary, but much of his fame rests on his Madonnas, found in many Venetian churches. The theme may be the same but the treatment varies so much that the viewer is constantly surprised by the imaginative power and sensitivity of this giant of Italian painting. No other Venetian had so much influence: Dürer came to study under him and Giorgione and Titian owe him an inestimable debt.

For his works, visit: Accademia, Museo Correr, San Zaccaria, Frari, SS. Giovanni e Paolo, Madonna dell'Orto, San Giovanni Crisostomo, Pinacoteca Querini–Stampalia, San Salvatore, Franchetti Gallery, and San Pietro Martire in Murano.

Carpaccio, Vittore (*c.* 1460-1525)
Like his master Gentile Bellini, Carpaccio specialized in large-scale paintings of Venetian life. No one else has depicted in such detail the canals, gondolas, bridges, houses and people of the early 1500s. He did a great deal of work for the *scuole*, the lay devotional associations which placed orders with him for great narrative cycles: *Scenes from the Life of Saint George, Saint Trythonius and Saint Jerome* and the *Legend of Saint Ursula.* An excellent portraitist who could create a mystery laden with poetry (*The Courtesans*), he mastered the problem of space and drew on humanist culture to give objects a symbolic value.

For his works, visit: Accademia, Museo Correr, Scuola San Giorgio della Schiavoni, Franchetti Gallery, San Domenico in Chiòggia.

Giorgione (real name: Giorgio da Castelfranco, *c.* 1477-1510)
Tragically, this disciple of Giovanni Bellini and, in his use of color, of Carpaccio, died of the plague just before his 30th birthday. So great was his influence on his friend Titian, Sebastiano del Piombo and others that, for centuries, critics were unsure which works were by him. It is now accepted that he is the chief creator of a small number of outstanding paintings, including *Portrait of a Young Man* (Berlin), *The Three Philosophers* (Vienna), and *The Tempest* (Accademia). His choice of esoteric themes, the richness of his color effects and his use of light and shade were important factors in his success.

For his works, visit: Accademia, Franchetti Gallery.

Detail from Gentile Bellini's Procession on the Piazza di S. Marco
(Accademia Gallery).

Lotto, Lorenzo (1480-1556)
A contemporary of Titian, Lotto was far too independent-minded to adopt his style – a crime of *lèse-majesté*! – while his erratic, strange, excessively sensitive nature could not accept the official piety of his day. His native city turned against him, so that he had to seek a livelihood elsewhere – in Rome, Bergamo, Jesi and Loretto where he died in poverty. Living in exile did not prevent this admirer of Giovanni Bellini and of Leonardo da Vinci from producing some of the finest Italian religious paintings and portraits.
For his works, visit: Accademia, SS. Giovanni e Paolo, San Giacomo dell'Orio, Museo Correr, I Carmini.

Titian (real name: Tiziano Vecellio, *c.* 1488-1576)
Titian, who studied under Giovanni Bellini with Giorgione, survived his fellow student by 66 years! His long life was well filled: frescoes, portraits both of men and women, self-portraits, mythological and religious scenes – all executed with equal success. He was greatly renowned, and painted the portraits of all the crowned heads of Europe and treated them as equals. As the ennobled official painter of the Republic, he was bold enough to refuse Pope Leo X's invitation to go to Rome. If we were to try to summarize his style, we might use three words: light, movement, power. He was the inventor of the halo effect and gave priority to color over form. Naturally, over three-quarters of a century, his style evolved; he changed from a style close to Gior-

gione's – in some cases, it is not easy to assess their individual contributions – to the aristocratic impersonality apparent in his portraits of Charles V. In the final years of his life, he produced religious paintings of overwhelming sadness. He was as famous for his genius as for his determination to find outlets for his works, which is why they are found in almost every church and museum in Venice.

For his works, visit: Accademia, Frari, Santa Maria della Salute, Franchetti Gallery, San Sebastiano, San Salvatore, Palace of the Doges, Libreria Marciana, I Gesuiti.

Tintoretto (real name: Jacopo Robuşti, 1518-1594)
Titian was an aristocrat, Tintoretto a man of the people. This passionate artist and admirer of Michelangelo rejected intellectual experimentation and the constraints of form in order to give free reign to his instinct. Similarly, he abandoned Graeco-Roman Antiquity for biblical subjects which were easier for simple people to understand.

"His originality," wrote Diego Valeri, "resides in his dramatic – indeed tragic – use of light and shade, in the struggle between day and night which Tuscan artists only saw as a dialectical opposition. The real drama was to be found in the atmosphere of the times because the wonder-filled summer of the Renaissance was already turning into an exquisitely corrupt autumn punctuated by storms of anguish. The poet Tasso was expressing at the same time in almost definitive terms that new state of mind with a line of verse which has become deservedly famous: *l'aspra tragedia dello stato umano* – the bitter tragedy of the human condition."

Tintoretto's fiery spirit is evident in his style and in the extent of his production: if a painter's greatness were measured by the number of paintings produced, no one could deny him the first prize!

For his works, visit: Accademia, Scuola di San Rocco, Palace of the Doges, Franchetti Gallery, San Giorgio Maggiore, Santa Maria della Salute, San Zaccaria, Madonna dell'Orto, San Moisè, Santa Maria Zobenigo (del Giglio), San Stefano, I Gesuati, San Trovaso, San Cassiano, San Rocco, Libreria Marciana, Museo Correr, I Gesuiti, San Pietro Martire in Murano.

Veronese (real name: Paolo Caliari, 1528-1588)
In contrast to the tormented atmosphere which dominates Tintoretto's work, Veronese's paintings were much more serene. Unequaled in his handling of color, he succeeded in obtaining contrasts in tones of light, whereas Tintoretto used deep shadows to achieve his bold contrasts. Diego Valeri wrote that Veronese devoted himself to "the cult of color expressing the universe's joy and splendor", insisting on a "clarity of

tints, on the pearly transparency of the penumbras, the crystalline depth of space, and the magic evanescence of the backgrounds". In his paintings, even when dealing with biblical subjects, he always put luxury and beauty before religious fervor. He was the painter *par excellence* of Venetian splendor.

For his works, visit: Accademia, SS. Giovanni e Paolo, San Sebastiano, Palace of the Doges, Libreria Marciana, San Giacomo dell'Orio, San Pietro Martire in Murano.

Tiepolo, Giambattista (1696-1770)
The 17th century may not have produced many great painters, but the 18th blazed with great names; Venice could lay claim to the landscape painters Canaletto and Guardi, the genre painter Pietro Longhi, and the great fresco painter Tiepolo. The latter was inspired by the work of Veronese and especially by his mastery of color and composition. Skilled in *trompe l'œil*, Tiepolo manipulated space as he wished, earning the admiration of all for his decorated ceilings. Equally at ease with pathos, he depicted Venice's *joie de vivre* at a time when the city was one of the most joyful of Europe, the home of Goldoni and of the Carnival.
For his works, visit: Accademia, Pinacoteca Querini–Stampalia, SS. Apostoli, Gli Scalzi, I Gesuati, Scuola Grande dei Carmini, San Polo, Palazzo Labia, San Stae, Ca' Rezzonico, Pietà, San Lazzaro degli Armeni, Duomo at Chiòggia, Villa Pisani on the Brenta, Villa Valmarana near Vicenza.

Canaletto (real name: Antonio Canal, 1697-1768)
It is said that Canaletto was the inventor of the postcard. Indeed this great landscape painter drew a good part of his income from his views of Venice which foreign visitors were quick to snap up. He also spent several years in London where he continued, along the banks of the Thames, with the experiments he had begun along the Grand Canal. When in Venice, the Piazza San Marco, the Rialto bridge, the church of the Salute, the great feasts and pageants, were subjects he tirelessly worked on: his technique of painting in the open air, of expressing the poetic atmosphere of his city, foreshadows the French school of the next century. His eye, attentive to the slightest detail, makes him a valuable witness of Venetian life.
For his works, visit: Accademia.

Longhi, Pietro (1702-1785)
Another witness of his time, Pietro Longhi takes us inside buildings. His scenes of daily life, often with a touch of satire, vividly recreate a throng of artisans, dancers, courtesans, bourgeois types and ecclesiastics, working, scheming and relaxing. Although his technique

varied very little – the size of almost all his canvases is the same – he produced small masterpieces of imaginative interpretation.

For his works, visit: Accademia, Museo Correr, Pinacoteca Querini-Stampalia, Palazzo Rezzonico.

Guardi, Francesco (1712-1792)
Guardi, who was Tiepolo's brother-in-law, tried his hand at every genre but his landscapes made him famous. His views of Venice take up the same themes as Canaletto – buildings, perspectives, regattas – but he displayed a liveliness of line and color beyond that of his contemporary who was more a delicate poet of reality. Guardi, an extremely prolific artist, did a great deal to popularize the image of Venice throughout Europe.

For his works, visit: Accademia, Museo Correr, Franchetti Gallery, Palazzo Rezzonico, San Angelo Raffaele.

VENICE
IN THE INDUSTRIAL AGE

Venice, today, is an urban administrative unit comprising the historic city, the islands of the lagoon and the mainland suburbs of *Marghera* and *Mestre*, the population of which exceeds that of the city.

ECONOMIC GROWTH ON THE LAGOON

Thanks to its port, the City of the Doges has been able to maintain itself while preserving and later developing its sea trade with Europe and the eastern Mediterranean. The geographical location of Venice enables it to outstrip all its rivals in the Middle-Eastern passenger trade.

The growth of the oil transportation trade and of industry in general led, after World War II, to saturation of the port's facilities. This made it necessary to extend shipping lanes across the lagoon to *Marghera*, the site of Italy's largest refinery and of the gigantic Montedison chemical and steel complex. Even this solution soon proved inadequate because ships of more than 16,530 tons/15,000 tonnes could not use the old waterway that runs from the Lido to the mainland through the San Marco basin and the *Giudecca* canal. There was no other alternative than to widen and deepen the *Malamocco* narrows, south of the *Lido*. Larger tankers could use this new route along the southern part of the lagoon across to the mainland, to the new port just south of Marghera.

Unfortunately, the major works involved in developing this industrial zone and the increasing activity of the surrounding factories threatened the survival of the historic city. The obvious question that comes to mind is: by adapting to the needs of the modern era, is Venice not, in fact, committing suicide? The struggle against the elements, the salty air and the rise in the sea level was already more than the financial and technical resources of the city could cope with. Widening the pass between the sea and the lagoon increased the damage caused by the normal action of tides and waves. Worse still, pollution from the chemical factories affects not only the stones and bricks of the buildings, but also the masterpieces by Venetian painters. Action to save the monuments and the works of art of the City of the Doges consequently conflicts with the industrial needs of Venice's mainland dependencies.

Establishing a balance between the two has brought a radical change in policies. In 1981, the authorities shelved plans to facilitate sea traffic through the *Malamocco* narrows, preferring instead to limit the depth to 39 ft/12 m which would effectively bar the way to the larger oil tankers and coal carriers, the draft of which exceeds that figure. The industrial zone of *Marghera* would be linked by oil pipelines to ships anchored outside, and there would be no need for any oil terminals inside the lagoon.

Meanwhile, until these major projects are completed, other measures can help to reduce the effects of the tides, such as deepening some of the canals, consolidating the banks and rebuilding the shoreline. Some 9900 acres/4000 hectares would be affected by these projects, of which 247 acres/100 hectares would be allocated for expansion of port facilities.

SEA LEVELS AND SUBSIDENCE: TWO ENEMIES RETREAT

As the earth's temperature rises, the ice caps melt and the level of the oceans is higher. This phenomenon adds to the complex effects of the tides and the winds, complicating the struggle against the ravages of water. Even more critical is the subsidence due to heavy buildings slowly sinking into the soil and the weakening of their foundations resulting from the wakes of ships. The propellers create a suction effect on the soil into which piles were once driven.

After the great floods of 1966, 1968, 1969 and 1979, Venice is haunted by a fear of the *acqua alta*, the high water it has always lived with and which is, in fact, necessary for the city's hygiene. There are times, though, when that high water spells danger. Brought about by a conjunction of high tides, high winds and an abnormal oscillation of the northern Adriatic basin caused by irregular and little understood currents, it is difficult to control.

The solution currently favored (a UNESCO program) involves closing the lagoon's three outlets with barriers which would come into operation the moment a tide exceeded 4 feet/1.2 m. Lower tides would be controlled by small sea-walls along the quays and at the entrance of waterways.

VENICE: A NEW ATLANTIS?

All this is still too simple. The hydrographers reckon that a strong south wind (the *sirocco*) could prevent the tide from ebbing, which could mean a much higher water level at the next high tide. Furthermore, an unexpected fall in atmospheric pressure could raise the sea level by another 4-18 in/10-45 cm: the *acqua alta* would become an *acqua altissima*! It is possible, consequently, to predict that Venice could be submerged if appropriate measures are not taken during the next 10 years but the lessons of history are there to calm our worst fears. According to UNESCO's report listing major floods, all the islands in the lagoon were submerged around the year 840, and water rose through the *calli* up to a man's height on September 23, 1240. In fact, the city almost disappeared on 50 different occasions from its early days to the middle of the 19th century but it survived.

Saving Venice is a Herculean task but modern technology should enable man to win the battle: by injecting cement, by using that amazingly resistant material, pre-stressed concrete, the subsidence of several buildings (notably the basilica of San Marco) has been stopped. Even if the dual effects of subsidence and of a rising water level can be held in check, what is even more urgent is the protection against damp and against chemical pollution of the stones of Venice, the plaster covering the walls and the works of art.

CATASTROPHIC POLLUTION

The effects of water and damp are compounded by the pollutants produced by home heating, the factories of *Marghera* and *Mestre* and by the ceaseless boat traffic through the canals. These chemical pollutants eat into the stone and marble which are already attacked by the bacteria-laden rising humidity; they break up or alter the colors of the paintings (especially greens and blues) and cause the varnish to turn yellow, so that paintings awaiting restoration display a chromatic imbalance. Diesel-burning heating systems have now been banned from Venice and municipal subsidies have helped householders to convert to methane.

A comprehensive set of atmospheric pollution controls has been established across the entire lagoon; buildings on the island of *San Servolo* are used for training craftsmen specializing in restoration work. The International Fund for Monuments has built a large restoration research laboratory. A number of research projects are being undertaken, ranging from the typology of Venice's historic center to the analysis of the various plasters used on the facades of the *palazzi*. Furthermore; there are training courses on the restoration of stonework.

Nobody will be surprised to learn that the pigeons, who form part of the charm and the liveliness of the Piazza di San Marco, do considerable damage to the buildings. This problem had taken on serious proportions because so many church roofs were in a state of disrepair and offered excellent roosting places for growing numbers of these birds. The roofs have been repaired to counter this particular menace.

GREATER VENICE NOT SO VENETIAN AFTER ALL?

The ancient city is thus making great efforts to save its inheritance. A haven of peace, Venice is the home of the middle-class and of artisans. The few troublemakers who sometimes give extra work to policemen on night duty prefer to live on the island of La Giudecca. Venice's economy is based on tourism and small businesses but the city's ambition is to become one of Italy's chief industrial and commercial centers by developing its mainland suburbs. Venice is close to reaching its goal but, as a result, it is no longer entirely Venetian: of the 350,000 inhabitants of greater Venice, only 90,000 live in the old city. Marghera and Mestre seek immigrant labor from the surrounding countryside and executives from inland cities as far away as Milan. Although Venice has a School of Architecture and the University of *Ca' Foscari*, the great technical colleges are situated in Milan and Rome. Furthermore, the capital necessary for the growth of Venetian industries does not come from Venice. Consequently, the city is forced to look inwards and to live in a conservative atmosphere. Saving Venice

World concern over the threat to Venice's survival has given rise to a wide-ranging program of restoration which is being undertaken through UNESCO, the Council of Europe, the European Cultural Foundation and various national Committees for the Preservation of Venice.

and preserving ancient traditions is not the same thing as living in the past when you consider how much imagination and how many superhuman and technical efforts are needed. No one can fail to recognize that saving Venice is one of the great human challenges of our time.

A BETTER CITY TO LIVE IN

The younger generation is moving from Venice to the mainland because of the city's housing crisis. Two new suburbs have been built at the two extremities of Venice – one on the island of *Sacca Fisola*, at the end of *La Giudecca*, the other on *Sant'Elena* near the Arsenale – but they have already reached saturation point. It would appear that the current policy of controlling rents and setting them at a figure owners consider too low, causes them to refuse to rent out their houses or apartments in the hope of selling them at prices beyond the reach of most residents. Venice has been overbuilt in terms of the original concept which depended on a careful balance of houses and gardens. There is no alternative to an overall reduction in the number of buildings in years to come. Living conditions cannot be improved adequately without bringing back the green spaces which once took up almost half the total area. This is all the more urgent in that the lack of trees worsens the impact of pollution; too many landscaped backyards and too many gardens have been sacrificed to the growth of the city itself.

UNESCO (no doubt to set an example) has donated 50 million lire to the city council for a relocation project in the *Ca' di Dio*.

THE MERRY-GO-ROUND OF THE VAPORETTI

A mere glance at the flow of pedestrians on any street shows that Venetians are great walkers. The reason is that the motorboats, even the semi-direct services, are far too slow – it was necessary to restrict their speed to 5 miles/8 km per hour to avoid damaging the foundations of the houses and the *palazzi*. In addition, to reach the mainland, the Venetian has to take a *vaporetto* to the station or to the *Piazzale Roma*, or go there on foot, in order to take the train or the bus for a trip lasting 30 minutes on average. This broken journey is another reason why the workers have moved to the new suburbs.

Several solutions have been put forward for these transport problems. Some have been accepted, like the increase in the number of ferry services; others rejected, like the plan which would have brought cars into the very heart of Venice by extending the *Cavallino* bridge by means of a motorway running alongside the *Fondamente Nuove.*

Two other proposals were seriously considered but, fortunately, they were turned down because of their enormous cost: an underground train running beneath the lagoon and an elevated monorail on pylons running from the mainland to the Lido.

The immediate solution has been a reorganization of the urban transport system, merging road and waterborne services in the *Azienda del Consorzio Trasporti Vene-ziano* (A.C.T.V.). Meanwhile the future of Venice and its surrounding districts hangs in an uneasy balance, with the advocates of industrial development on one side and, on the other, those who give priority to the cultural and tourist potential of the city. The point of view of this second group is of course, diametrically opposed to those who have to shoulder the blame for an atmospheric pollution which personally affects many people, including the tourists, at various times depending on weather conditions. It is feared that the air of Venice could become as polluted as it already is in *Fusina* and on the *Riviera del Brenta.*

AMENITIES IN VENICE

Venice, built on an archipelago comprising 117 islands large and small, is divided into six districts (*sestieri*): San Marco, Castello, Cannaregio, Santa Croce, San Polo and Dorsoduro.

Houses in each district are sequentially numbered irrespective of the street they are in – thus 1141 on the Zattere does not mean there are at least 1141 numbers along that quay, but simply that this is the 1141st numbered building of the Dorsoduro district. Don't be surprised if you find a four-digit number in a street with just 10 buildings.

The streets are paved with stone or brick. Some are public streets, others belong to the residents but you may use them freely even though they are technically private alleyways.

There are several types of street in Venice: the *calle* which is a former pathway, the *salizzada* (paved street), the *rio terra* (a former waterway filled in to give greater strength to the buildings), the *ramo* (a little passage), the *sottoportico* (usually under an arcade), the *lista* (a limited access way leading to an ambassadorial residence, lined with white slabs which mark the limits of diplomatic immunity).

▬ TRAVEL IN VENICE

The motorboats are slow and, in spite of their frequency and the pleasure you gain from cruising through a city instead of driving, you will soon realize that the best way to see Venice is on foot. The main walks are well

Palace of the Doges: the Giant's Staircase.

signposted, and you risk getting lost only if you wander away from them. This is why we offer you in a later section of this book a range of walks through Venice. These walks lead to museums, churches and palaces you would be well advised to visit but, for a pause, you will be happy enough to take a motorboat from time to time. That is why we have shown, next to the main points of interest in each walk (buildings, museums, hotels, restaurants, cafés) the nearest landing stage of the appropriate motor barge service. This has an added advantage for visiting those sights of Venice that warrant a half-day visit, when you may prefer to go straight there by water transport.

Waterbuses or Vaporetti?

The terminology of Venice's water transport system is fairly complex. The different types of boats that criss-cross the lagoon, and chug along the canals, all have their distinctive names. Apart from the gondolas, the first boats were the *vaporetti* (1860).

What non-Venetians may simply call motorboats can be *vaporetti* (small waterbuses), *motoscafi* (smaller and with a lower waterline), *motonavi* (the biggest of all with a bridge and a smokestack), *traghetti* (small or large ferries) for crossing the Grand Canal and for taking your car from *Tronchetto* to the *Lido*; or the *motobatelli* which will take you from *San Pietro in Volta* to *Chiòggia*.

You will probably use the *vaporetto*, Line 1, most frequently. This offers an *accelerato* service, i.e. an omnibus service, from *Piazzale Roma* to the *Lido* by way of the Grand Canal and the San Marco basin; you will also use the No. 2 Line *motoscafo* which provides a *diretto* (read "semi-direct") service between the *Rialto*, the station and the *Lido* by way of the *Rio Nuovo*. But don't be misled – the *accelerati* are always slower.

Regarding Fares

Remember that the *motoscafo* will cost you 60% more than a *vaporetto* by day and double at night. Monthly, weekly and even day tourist passes (about 10,000 lire), allowing you to travel anywhere, are available; enquire at the A.C.T.V. Riva degli Schiavoni, opposite the San Zaccaria landing stage. The *vaporetti* are more comfortable and offer a better view: they are the most suitable for seeing the Grand Canal.

Boat stops are situated at the various *pontili* (landing stages) most of which have a ticket-selling booth. Where there is no booth (i.e. at some *vaporetti* stops) you can obtain your ticket on board, but it is advisable to buy a ticket before boarding whenever possible or you run the risk of a surcharge. Tender the exact fare, or be patient and you will eventually get your change. Among the notices pinned up on the landing stages you will find the boat timetables as well as information about the tides.

The boat reverses a little to loosen the mooring ropes, and you're off along an aquatic street. The skill of the man handling the rope is worth watching – it is as impressive as that of the "captain" who occasionally steers the boat with his feet! Also note the expression of two skippers passing each other when one of them has reached the landing stage ahead of the other... !

The Main Waterbus Routes

1 – (vaporetto accelerato) *Piazzale Roma* (S. Chiara), *Ferrovia* (S. Lucia), *Riva di Biasio, S. Marcuola, S. Stae* (Ca' Pesaro), *Ca' d'Oro, Rialto, S, Silvestro, S. Angelo, S. Toma* (Frari), *Ca' Rezzonico, Accademia, S. M. del Giglio, S. M. della Salute, S. Marco* (Vallaresso), *S. Zaccaria* (Jolanda), *Arsenale, Giardini, S. Elena, Lido* (S. M. Elisabetta).

2 – (motoscafo diretto) *Rialto, Ferrovia* (Scalzi), *Piazzale Roma* (Rio Nuovo), *S. Samuele, Accademia, S. Marco* (Vallaresso), *S. Zaccaria* (Danieli), *Giardini* (during the exhibition), *S. Elena, Lido* (S. M. Elisabetta, as far as the Casino only during the summer).

4 – (vaporetto diretto, June to September only) *Piazzale Roma* (S. Chiara), *Ferrovia* (Scalzi), *Rialto, Accademia, S. Marco* (Vallaresso), *S. Zaccaria* (Danieli), *Lido* (S. M. Elisabetta).

5 – (motoscafo, round trip in both directions, *circolare destra* and *circolare sinstra*) *Fondamenta Venier* (Murano), *Serenella, Museo* (Murano), *Navagero* (Murano), *Faro* (Murano), *Colonna* (Murano), *Cimitero* (S. Michele), *Fondamenta Nuove, Ospedale Civile, Celestia, Campo della Tana, S. Zaccaria* (Jolanda), *S. Giorgio, Zitelle* (Giudecca), *Redentore* (Giudecca), *S. Eufemia* (Giudecca), *Zattere* (Ponte Longo), *S. Basilio* (Marittima), *Sacca Fisola, Silos, S. Marta, Piazzale Roma, Ferrovia* (Bar Roma), *Ponte Guglie, Ponte Tre Archi, S. Alvise, Madonna dell'Orto, Fondamenta Nuove, Cimitero* (S. Michele), *Colonna* (Murano), *Faro* (Murano), *Navagero* (Murano), *Museo* (Murano).

6 – (motonave diretta) direct service between the Lido and the Riva degli Schiavoni, Paglia landing stage.

11 – (motonave) *Venice* (Riva degli Schiavoni), *Lido* (S. M. Elisabetta), *Pellestrina, Chiòggia:* the journey takes 1 hr 30 mins. altogether; only during the season.

12 – (motonave) *Fondamenta Nuove, Murano* (Faro), *Mazzorbo, Burano, Torcello.*

17 – (nave traghetto: car ferry) *Piazzale Roma* (Tronchetto), *Lido* (S. Nicolò), *Punta Sabbioni.*

28 – (motoscafo direttissimo) *Piazzale Roma, S. Zaccaria* (by Rio Nuovo), *Municipal Casino.*

34 – (vaporetto diretto) *Tronchetto, Lido, S. Marco*, only during the summer season.

Gondolas and Taxis

You will find many other types of boats in Venice: small motor barges, often painted in vivid colors, *maone, caorline, sandoli* and *topi*; motor pleasure boats in varnished wood, *motoscafi* (the name is also applied to the motorboats of the A.C.T.V. used for the direct services) owned by private individuals, firms or public bodies. The police, the army (not just the navy) and the post office, all use motorboats. Some, painted black and yellow, are motor hearses...

If you want to avoid the crowds on public motorboats, you can hire the *taxi acquei*, splendid launches in varnished wood.

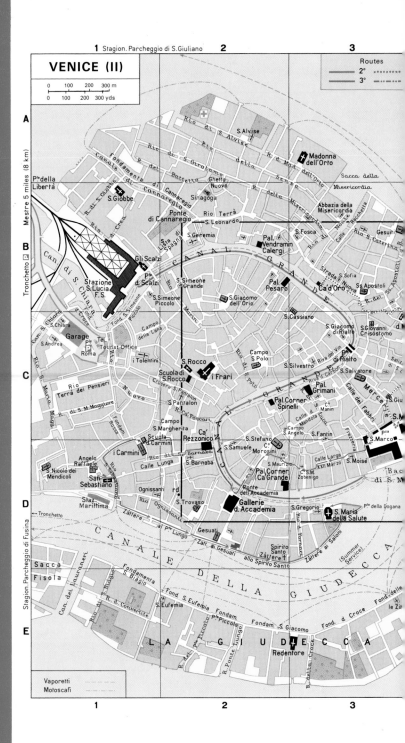

VENICE (II)

Routes
2° ....
3° ....

0   100   200   300 m
0   100   200   300 yds

A

B

C

D

E

Mestre 5 miles (8 km)

Tronchetto

Stagion. Parcheggio di Fusina

Vaporetti
Motoscafi

Stagion. Parcheggio di S.Giuliano

Rio di S. Alvise
S.Alvise
R. d. Mad.
Madonna dell'Orto
Sacca della Misericordia
Fondamenta Canale di Cannaregio
R. del Battello
Ghetto Nuovo
R. della Sensa
R. della Misericordia
Canale di Cannaregio
S.Giobbe
R. d. S. Girolamo
Sinagoga
Abbazia della Misericordia
Ponte di Cannaregio
Rio Terrà
S.Leonardo
S.Fosca
Gesuiti
Rio di S. Caterina
P.ta della Libertà
Can. di S. Chiara
Gli Scalzi
S.Geremia
CANALE GRANDE
Pal. Vendramin Calergi
Strada di S.Sofia
Ss.Apostoli
Stazione S.Lucia F.S.
P.te d.Scalzi
S.Simeone Grande
S.Simeone Piccolo
S.Giacomo dell'Orio
Pal. Pesaro
Ca'd'Oro
R. del
Fond. S. Simeone Piccolo
Marin
S.Cassiano
S.Giacomo di Rialto
S.Giovanni Crisostomo
Garage p.le Roma
Tourist Office
Campo della Lana
i Tolentini
Crosera S. Pantalon
S.Rocco
Scuola di S.Rocco
i Frari
Rio di S. Polo
Campo S.Polo
S.Silvestro
Riva del Vin
di Rialto
S.Salvatore
Merceria
S.Andrea
Rio Terrà dei Pensieri
Rio Nuovo
S.Pantalon
R. d. Foscari
Pal. Grimani
Riva di Carbon
Calle del Fabbri
Giu
Rio di S. M. Maggiore
Fondam. Rezzo
Campo S.Margherita
Ca' Rezzonico
Pal. Corner Spinelli
Calle d. Mandola
C. Manin
S.M.
S.Marco
Scuola d.Carmini
i Carmini
Rio di S. Barnaba
S.Barnaba
S.Stefano
C° Morosini
S.Samuele
Campo S.Angelo
S.Fantin
Frezzeria
Angelo Raffaele
Calle Lunga
S.Maurizio
C.S.M. Zobenigo
XXII Marzo
S.Moisè
S.Nicolò dei Mendicoli
San Sebastiano
Ognissanti rd
S.Trovaso
Pal. Corner Ca'Grande
Calle Larga
S.Moisè
Bac di S.M
Staz. Marittima
Ponte dell'Accademia
Gallerie d. Accademia
S.Gregorio
S.Maria della Salute
P.ta della Dogana
Zattere
Zatt. al P.te Lungo
Gesuati
Zatt. ai Gesuati
allo Spirito Santo
Spirito Santo
Zattere ai Saloni
(Summer Service)
CANALE DELLA GIUDECCA
Sacca Fisola
Fondamenta S.Biagio
Can. dei Lavraneri
S.Eufemia
Fond S.Eufemia
Fondam S.Giacomo
Fond. d. Croce
Fond. delle le Zit
R. d. Convertite
P.ta Piccolo
LA GIUDECCA
P.ta Ponte Lungo
Redentore
Calle Croce

1   **2**   **3**

In addition to our detailed itineraries,

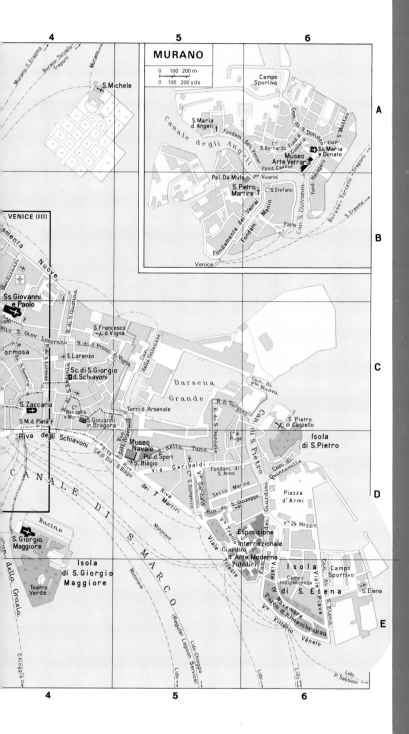

the routes shown on this map are also interesting.

They carry a maximum of four passengers and are quite expensive but they are useful for getting from the *Piazzale Roma* or the station to your hotel or the *Lido.*

There are also *portabagagli* who will take your luggage to your hotel for a reasonable price.

But of course, the most popular boat is the gondola, which is descended from the early flat-bottomed boats used in the lagoon. You can cross the Grand Canal in one (*traghetto*) or take one wherever you want to go by day or night. The musical accompaniment is optional.

The rates are very expensive, but the journeys are memorable. You should book through a travel agency, or at least agree on a fare before setting foot in the boat.

The gondola is a large flat-bottomed boat with a gracefully curved stem and stern. It is asymmetrical because it is propelled by a single oar at the back on the starboard (right) side. Probably the most beautiful boat in the world, it is extremely stable and maneuverable. It used to be painted in bright colors until 1562, when a senatorial edict ordered it to be painted black to put an end to the increasingly lavish decoration by which certain citizens underscored their importance.

The prow (*prova*) is decorated with a piece of metal (*ferro*) shaped like a six-toothed comb (*pettine*) symbolizing the six *sestieri* of Venice; the upper tooth extends at the back into a seventh tooth, representing the *Dorsoduro* district and the island of *La Giudecca* which form a single *sestiere.* In the middle of some gondolas, a small cloth (*felze*) provides shelter for the passengers. A gondola is some 36 ft/11 m in length overall, 6 ft/1.75 m wide, weighs 1100 pounds/500 kg and costs several million lire.

▬ PLANNING YOUR STAY

To visit Venice, you will combine walking with water transport; if you enjoy walking you will probably use fewer motorboats but remember that these are essential for a good view of the Grand Canal.

Incidentally, if you have shoe trouble, like a broken heel, there is a quick repair service at Calle della Fava 5188 (Map III C-4 boat service 1,2 or 4: Rialto).

To help you avoid getting lost, we suggest that you follow the main signposted routes which link *Piazza di San Marco* with the *Rialto*, the railway station, the *Accademia, SS. Giovanni e Paolo*, and the *Fondamenta Nuove*, as well as the *Rialto* to the *Accademia.* These routes will bring you to, or near, all the important sites and buildings, and they will enable you to find, by referring to your map, centers of interest that may be situated a little off the route. If, at any time, you do get lost, the locals will be pleased to help you. Because Venice is relatively small, you will eventually arrive at somewhere you know. Campaniles make useful landmarks. Route indications and signs to the nearest landing stages are on the walls at street corners.

Venice in One Day

If you are spending a day in Venice, we recommend that you go from *Piazzale Roma* or the *Santa Lucia* station to the *San Zaccaria* landing stages by *vaporetto* (No. 1, direction Lido). You will travel along the Grand Canal★★★ and view the Campanile,★★ the Basilica of San Marco★★★ and the Palace of the Doges★★★ from the lagoon. Then, after walking through the *Piazza*★★ and the *Piazzetta*★★ and seeing the basilica, you can go on to the *Rialto*★ by way of the *Mercerie* which begins under the clock tower (*see arrow "Rialto"*). Crossing the bridge you will reach *Santa Maria Gloriosa dei Frari*★★ (paintings by Bellini and Titian) and the *Scuola Grande di San Rocco*★★ (masterpieces by Tintoretto). You will then have no trouble in getting back to the station or the *Piazzale Roma* on foot or by taking the *vaporetto* at the *San Tomà* landing stage (*arrow "Al vaporetto" on yellow signs*).

A Weekend in Venice

In two days, you can complement the above one-day program as follows: from *Piazza di San Marco,*★★ spend a half-day visiting *SS. Giovanni e Paolo*★★ (13th century apse, Bellini polyptych), the *Colleoni* equestrian statue, the *Scuola di San Marco* (early Renaissance marble facade), *San Giorgio degli Schiavoni*★ (Carpaccio paintings) and *San Zaccaria*★ (G. Bellini and Tintoretto). In the afternoon, leaving from the *San Zaccaria* landing stage, go to the island of *San Giorgio Maggiore*★★ (classical masterpiece by Palladio, Tintoretto paintings in the church). Take the boat to the *Zattere* and visit the church of the *Gesuati* on the quay (Tiepolo ceiling), the *Accademia* gallery★★ where you will see about 10 of the finest paintings in the world, including Giorgione's *Tempest*. Finally, visit the *Santa Maria della Salute*★★, a masterpiece of Baroque art. The boat will then take you back to the station or to *San Marco*.

A Week in Venice

Spend five or six days in Venice and one or two on the islands. Decide what itineraries to follow according to your taste and your wishes because the routes you follow depend on where you are staying. Your timetable will also depend on the length of your visits to particular museums and other buildings.

Furthermore, the detailed information given earlier on the boat services, and on the signposted walks, will enable you to choose your own rhythm and themes for your exploration of Venice. You should note that you can visit the islands of *Murano,*★ *Torcello*★★ and *Burano* in one day (Murano in the morning, lunch at Torcello or Burano, a visit to both islands in the afternoon) and *San Michele* in half a day. The island of *San Giorgio Maggiore*★★ fits neatly into a city itinerary.

Do not be worried if you are on your own in Venice. You will always succeed in making yourself understood and you can stroll during the day and in the evening. Crime is not as common in Venice as in other Italian cities. Venice is a welcoming city, free from the paranoia of the great urban centers.

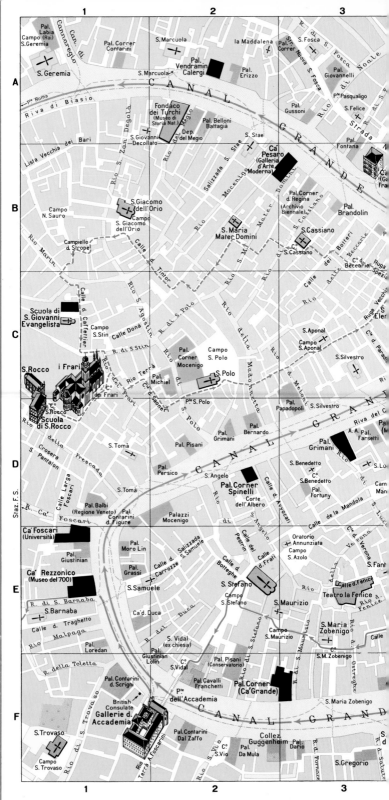

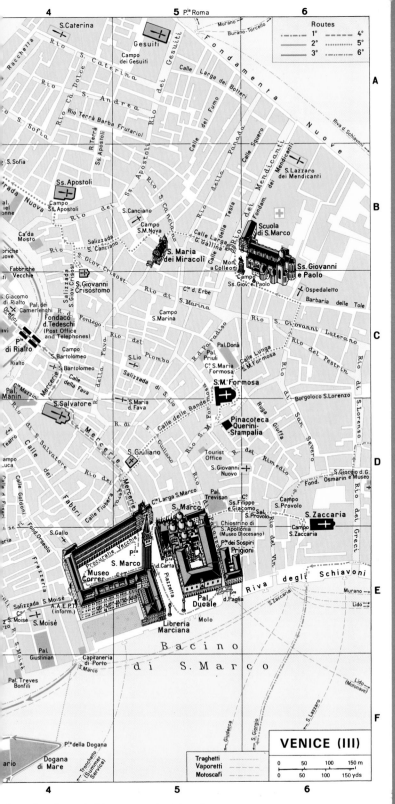

Strolls Through Venice

To make your sightseeing easier, we have divided Venice into six zones, each comprising a comfortable itinerary:

Zone A is devoted to the Grand Canal★★★ (p. 75).

Zone B is limited to the buildings around Piazza di San Marco★★ (p. 83).

Zone C is situated between San Marco and the *Zattere* and follows the signposted walk *San Marco* to the *Accademia*★★ (p. 101).

Zone D comprises the area covered by the signposted walks *San Marco* to the *Rialto*★ and the *Ferrovia* station (p. 112).

Zone E lies between the *Rialto*, the *Scuola Grande di San Rocco*★★ and the *Zattere* includes the signposted walks from the *Rialto* to the *Frari* and the *Accademia (p. 120)*.

Zone F is between *San Marco*, the *Riva degli Schiavoni* and the *Fondamenta Nuove* comprising the *Ospedale* (hospital) walk (p. 129).

In each zone you will find, grouped in a progessive logical sequence, not only the sites and buildings situated along the signposted walk, but also others that are in the immediate vicinity. Map references are given in brackets after each name so that you can locate them easily.

Three chapters are devoted to the islands of the Venetian lagoon, to the *Riviera del Brenta* and to the villas built by Palladio in the Vicenza district.

▬ ACCOMMODATION IN VENICE

Apart from the consideration of cost (Venice is regarded as an expensive city), your choice of hotel will depend on three factors. Do you want to stay near the railway station or your car? Do you prefer the historic city center? Do you feel attracted by the lagoon? If you decide on the historic center, you have the option of the waterfront (along the Grand Canal, the *Riva degli Schiavoni* or *La Giudecca*) or of an intimate corner of the old city, overlooking a *calle* or a quiet garden. Water, it is true, is an essential part of the Venetian scene but the motorboat engines are noisy, and even from the gondolas there are shouts and singing from the gondoliers. Behind the age-old facades, however, there are unsuspected havens of quiet and greenery.

Several hotels in the historic center offer you a choice between the lively spectacle of the canals and a view over a peaceful Mediterranean garden where only the birds sing. If you opt for the seashore or the lagoon, you can choose the *Lido*, *Torcello* or the island of *La Giudecca*.

A number of hotels are closed during the winter, or at least they shut their restaurants but those which remain open offer special prices from November 1 as part of an all-inclusive travel package (inquire at your travel agent or at airline offices). Remember that price increases occur several times a year and even during the season. It is possible therefore to have to pay more than the prices stated on official documents.

A last word of advice: unless you like taking risks, you are strongly urged to book at least one month ahead, either through a travel agent, or by phoning and sending a money order to cover the cost of one or two nights. For those who lack foresight, there are always the steps of the Santa Lucia railway station...

Hotels

For your greater convenience, the hotels of Venice are listed separately from those of the Lido and the islands.

▲▲▲▲**Bauer Grünwald** Map III E-F-4 (Lines 1, 2 or 4: S. Marco), Campo S. Moisè, 1459, tel. 707-022, telex 410075. 213 rooms, air cond., hairdresser. There are views overlooking S. Moisè, Rio dei Barcaroli and the Grand Canal. The largest hotel complex in Venice after the *Danieli*, this is one of the city's best hotels; the comfort and the service cannot be faulted. It is a world apart in a fashionable district. One has to recognize all these excellent qualities to forgive its massive modern facade which now overwhelms the Church of San Moisè and, on the other side, looks down on the splendid *palazzi* built on the Grand Canal.

▲▲▲▲**Cipriani** Map II E-4 (Lines 5 or 8: Zitelle, but preferably use the hotel's own boat), Giudecca, 10, tel. 707-744, telex 410162. 100 rooms, 7 suites, air cond., open-air swimming pool, Yves Saint-Laurent boutique, hairdresser. Motorboat at the *Piazzetta landing stage*, in front of *Harry's Bar*.
This is an exceptional site. Gardens on the edge of the lagoon, a seawater pool larger than Olympic size. The cuisine is the equal of *Harry's Bar*. Holiday living (sun-bathing, bathing, dancing) 3 mins. from the heart of Venice. The *Cipriani* is taking over an adjoining ducal palace. One of the finest panoramic views over Venice and the Piazza di San Marco can be seen from here. There are tennis facilities and a private marina.

▲▲▲▲**Danieli Royal Excelsior** Map III E-6 (Lines 1, 2 or 4: S. Zaccaria), Riva degli Schiavoni, 4196, tel. 26-480, telex 410077. 242 rooms, air cond, roof restaurant. Situated on the edge of San Marco basin, a stone's throw from the Palace of the Doges. This Venetian hotel *par excellence* was established in 1822 in the *Palazzo Dandolo*, a noble home of the late 14th century which served as the French Embassy. Luxurious interior decor, an abundance of marble, chandeliers, a staircase with arcades – in a word, a monument. There are three hotels in one: two buildings, which are part of the hotel, flank the palace to which they are linked by a footbridge. One of the buildings, a modern one, has a garden restaurant on its roof with a view over the lagoon beyond the island of *S. Giorgio Maggiore*. Celebrities who have stayed here include *Dickens*, *d'Annunzio*, and *Wagner*, as well as

George Sand and *Alfred de Musset* whose stormy love affair was carried on in Room 10...

▲▲▲▲**Gritti Palace Hotel** Map III F-3 (Line 1: S. Maria del Giglio, but you will probably use a *motoscafo-taxi*) Campo S. Maria del Giglio 2467, tel. 26-044, telex 410125. 91 rooms, air cond., hairdresser, restaurant on the Grand Canal.
Better than a hotel, a Gothic-style palace where you are welcomed as a guest and not just as a customer. The quiet atmosphere has appealed to many world celebrities who have stayed here, including *Hemingway, Simenon* and *Ruskin* who is said to have written part of *The Stones of Venice* while staying here. Splendid view over the Grand Canal and majestic *Santa Maria della Salute.*

▲▲▲**Etap Park Hotel** Map II C-1 (Line 2: Piazzale Roma), Fondamenta Condulmer, 245, tel. 52-85-394, telex 410310. 100 rooms, air cond. This is a haven of peace between a garden and a *rio*. It is close to the Piazzale Roma car park and near a motorboat station.

▲▲▲**Europa & Regina** Map III E-F-4 (Lines 1, 2 or 4: S. Marco), Calle Larga XXII Marzo, 2159, tel. 700-477, telex 410123. 155 rooms, air cond., overlooks the Grand Canal.
Another magnificent hotel, undeniably one of the best of those situated near the historic center but in a peaceful spot at the corner of the *Rio di S. Moisè* and the Grand Canal. This is one of the places which best corresponds to the traditional idea we have of Grand Canal Venice. It has a very pleasant restaurant opposite the church of *S. Maria della Salute*, the *Ristorante Terrazza Tiepolo.*

▲▲▲**Gabrielli Sandwirth** Map II D-4 (Line 1: Arsenale), Riva degli Schiavoni, 4110, tel. 52-31-580, telex 410228. 110 rooms, air cond., overlooks the San Marco basin and a small garden. Undeniably this is the hotel which best reflects Venetian traditions. An incomparable refuge for lovers of the past who can find here the atmosphere of the historic city. Its exceptional site – in the elbow of the quay just where the crowds thin out – allows it a view over *S. Giorgio Maggiore*, the Palace of the Doges and the Grand Canal.

▲▲▲**Locanda Cipriani** (on the island of Torcello, Map I, p. 15) tel. 730-150. 5 rooms only, air cond., well known restaurant. A holiday spot known throughout the world: secluded, calm, food served in the open or inside overlooking the garden according to the weather and season. Only five rooms, but what rooms! The refuge of famous artists and writers, the *Locanda* has numbered among its guests *Hemingway* in 1948 and, more recently, *Orson Welles, Sophia Loren, Margot Fonteyn, Virna Lisi, Roberto Rossellini, Bernard Buffet* and *Dorazio* – each the winner of a Venice Biennial – *V. Giscard d'Estaing* and Britain's *Queen Elizabeth*. Comfort is first-class, but in spite of its fame *La Locanda* remains a quiet, discreet residence. If you merely want to go for lunch, a *motoscafo* leaves daily at midday near *Harry's Bar*; it gets to Torcello 12.35 pm, then leaves at 3 pm and arrives back in Venice at 3.40 pm (it is wise to reserve in advance by telephone); reservations can also be made through *Harry's Bar* (52-36-797).

▲▲▲**Londra Palace** Map III E-6 (Lines 1, 2 or 4: S. Zaccaria, or 1: Arsenale), Riva degli Schiavoni, 4171, tel. 700-533, telex 431315. 67 rooms, air cond., overlooks S. Marco dock at the corner of *Rio di S. Antonin*. Views of the island of *S. Giorgio Maggiore* and *Punta della Dogana* which divides the Grand Canal from the Canal of *La Giudecca*.

▲▲▲**Luna** Map III E-4 (Lines 1, 2 or 4: S. Marco) Calle dell'Ascensione, 1243, tel. 89-840, telex 410236. 125 rooms, air cond., in the heart of the fashionable district. One of Venice's de luxe hotels with an excellent restaurant. Central, yet away from the crowds, it is one of the best hotels of its kind, and its great appeal lies in its comfort, its service and the welcome it offers, as well as its location – just behind the Grand Canal. You can reach it either by a small waterway where a special landing stage awaits you or by the luxurious *Calle Vallaresso*.

▲▲▲**Metropole** Map III E-6 (Lines 1, 2 or 4: S. Zaccaria), Riva degli Schiavoni, 4149, tel. 705-044, telex 410340. 64 rooms, air cond., facing the island of *S. Giorgio Maggiore*. Well worth a special mention. Entirely modernized and tastefully refurnished, it is now one of Venice's most comfortable hotels. Location comparable to that of the *Danieli*, a stone's throw from the church of *S. Zaccaria*.

▲▲▲**Monaco & Grand Canal** Map III F-4 (Lines 1, 2 or 4: S. Marco), Calle Vallaresso, 1325, tel. 700-211, telex 410450. 80 rooms, air cond., views overlooking the Grand Canal, *S. Maria della Salute*, the basin of S. Marco, and the *island of S. Giorgio Maggiore*. One of the best sites along the Canal, with a restaurant overlooking the water, the hotel is a couple of steps from the S. Marco landing stage, at the corner of one of the most fashionable *calli*, and in front of *Harry's Bar*. Undeniably the best hotel in Venice. No package tours; prices are reasonable.

▲▲▲**Saturnia e International** Map III E-3 (Lines 1, 2 or 4: S. Marco), Calle Larga XXII Marzo, 2398, tel. 708-377, telex 410355. 98 rooms, air cond., situated on a wide and elegant street between S. Marco and the Accademia bridge. This is a 14th-century *palazzo*, with private access for taxis and gondolas. There are two restaurants, the *Caravella* indoors and *Il Cortile* outdoors.

▲▲**Ala** Map III E-3 (Line 1: S. M. del Giglio), S. Maria del Giglio, 2494, tel. 708-333, telex 410275. 63 rooms, air cond. A quiet and pleasant hotel in a secluded corner of the Campo *S. Maria Zobenigo*, halfway between Piazza di S. Marco and the Accademia bridge. A recommended hotel with an adjoining restaurant, the *Ristorante Al Giglio*, which is one of the most pleasant in Venice.

▲▲**Bonvecchiati** Map III D-4 (Lines 1, 2 or 4: S. Marco), Calle Goldoni, 4488, tel. 52-85-017, telex 410560. 90 rooms, air cond. A typical Venetian hotel. The owners have made up for the relative gloominess of the location (the *calli* are very narrow) by decorating the hotel with a collection of modern paintings.

▲▲**Cavalletto e Doge Orseolo** Map III E-4 (Lines 1, 2 or 4: S. Marco), Calle Cavalletto 1107 (open from March to November), tel. 700-955, telex 410684. 81 rooms, air cond., facade faces the Orseolo basin. A hotel which truly "is" Venice – very close to the water, overlooking a fairly extensive basin where dozens of gondolas are moored, providing a typical Venetian atmosphere, enhanced by the shouts of the gondoliers who go to bed late and get up early. The hotel is 2 min. from Piazza di S. Marco.

▲▲**Concordia** Map III D-5 (Lines 1, 2 or 4: S. Marco or S. Zaccaria), Calle Larga di San Marco 367, tel. 706-866, telex 411069. 60 rooms, air cond. The nearest hotel to the basilica: the breakfast room looks out onto the north facade of S. Marco. Impeccable service. Rooms with modern bathrooms. An excellent restaurant across the road, the *Ristorante Antico Panada*, is associated with the hotel.

▲▲**Do Pozzi** Map III E-3 (Line 1: S. M. del Giglio; 1, 2 or 4: S. Marco), Corte do Pozzi 2373, tel. 707-855. 29 rooms, air cond. A comfortable hotel 300 m/320 yards from Piazza di S. Marco.

▲▲**Flora** Map III E-3 (Lines 1: S. M. del Giglio; 1, 2 or 4: S. Marco), Calle Bergamaschi, 2283/a, tel. 705-844. 36 rooms, air cond. The hotel is in a peaceful garden courtyard on the S. Marco to Accademia walk, not far from the theater *La Fenice*.

▲▲**Graspo de Uva** Map III C-4 (Lines 1, 2 or 4; Rialto), Calle dei Bombaseri 5094, tel. 52-23-647. 23 rooms, air cond. This hotel's main advantage is its restaurant, one of the best in Venice. Situated in the Rialto district, it is ideal accommodation for gastronomes.

▲▲**La Fenice e des Artistes** Map III E-3 (Line 1: S. M. del Giglio), Campiello Fenice, 1936, tel. 52-32-333, telex 411150. 58 rooms, air cond. Situated by the theater, this is one of the most charming hotels of the central area: quiet, water, shade and a delightful open-air restaurant.

▲▲**Malibran** Map III C-4 (Lines 1, 2 or 4: Rialto), S. Giovanni Crisostomo 5864, tel. 52-28-028. 29 rooms. A very well situated hotel near the *Malibran* theater and the Rialto bridge.

▲▲**Montecarlo** Map III D-5 (Lines 1, 2 or 4: S. Marco or S. Zaccaria), Calle degli Speccheri 463, tel. 707-144, telex 411098. 45 rooms. Another very well managed central hotel with an adjoining well patronized restaurant, the *Trattoria Ai do Forni*.

▲▲**Principe** Map II B-2 (Lines 1, 2 or 5: Ferrovia), Lista di Spagna 146, tel. 715-022, telex 410070. 156 rooms, air cond. Close to the station and beside the Grand Canal.

▲▲**Savoia e Jolanda** Map III E-6 (Lines 1, 2 or 4: S. Zaccaria), Riva degli Schiavoni 4187, tel. 706-644, telex 410275. 66 rooms. This is the only hotel in this category with the same view as the *Danieli*.

▲**American Hotel** Map II D-2 (Lines 1 or 2: Accademia; 5

or 8: Zattere), S. Vio 628, tel. 704-733, telex 410275. 30 rooms, situated on the Rio S. Vio. A very good hotel frequented by many Scandinavians. Located in one of the quietest parts of Venice, it offers the charm of a narrow quay along the *rio*, not far from the Guggenheim Foundation.

▲**Da Bruno** Map III C-5 (Lines 1, 2 or 4: Rialto), Salizzada S. Lio 5726/a, tel. 52-30-452. 32 rooms. Centrally situated, equidistant from *S. Maria Formosa, SS. Giovanni e Paolo*, the Rialto and Piazza di S. Marco.

▲**Firenze** Map III E-4 (Lines 1, 2 or 4: S. Marco), Salizzada S. Moisè 1490, tel. 52-22-858. 26 rooms. Another good hotel near S. Marco.

▲**Guerrini** Map II B-2 (Lines 1, 2 or 5: Ferrovia), Lista di Spagna 265, tel. 715-333. 34 rooms. A good hotel near the railway station.

▲**Iris** Map III D-1 (Line 1: S. Tomà), S. Tomà 2910/A, tel. 52-22-882. 25 rooms. Recommended for those who prefer peace and quiet to the lively quarter of S. Marco. Close to the *Frari*.

▲**Noemi** Map III D-4 (Lines 1, 2 or 4: S. Marco), Calle dei Fabbri 909, tel. 52-38-144. 15 rooms. A simple hotel but well recommended.

▲**San Fantin** Map III E-3 (Line 1: S. M. del Giglio), Campiello Fenice 19307/a, tel. 52-31-401. 14 rooms. One of the most pleasant districts of Venice; music lovers are only a couple of steps from *La Fenice* theater.

Pensiones in Venice

▲▲**Accademia-Villa Maravegie** Map III F-2 (Line 1 or 2: Accademia), Fondamenta Bollani 1058, tel. 52-37-846. 26 rooms, located opposite the *Accademia*, a few yards from the Grand Canal. Very well kept pensione in one of the most pleasant residential districts of Venice. Well located for the landing stage at Accademia bridge from where you can easily walk to the opposite bank. From there, San Marco and the Rialto are easily accessible.

▲▲**Ca'd'Oro** Map III B-3 (Line 1: Ca'd'Oro), Strada Nuova 4391/a tel. 52-34-797. 13 rooms, a couple of steps from the Grand Canal near the *Ca'd'Oro*, on the pedestrian route from the station to the Rialto and to S. Marco.

▲▲**La Calcina** Map II D-2 (Lines 1 or 2: Accademia, 5 or 8: Zattere), Zattere 780, tel. 706-466. 32 rooms, the facade is on the large Giudecca Canal, very good home cooking (fresh vegetables); lunch only. Family atmosphere. Situated on the *Gesuati* quay, at the corner of Rio S. Vio, *La Calcina* gets its name from the *Ponte Calcina* ("the bridge of lime"). It was originally a small bar and was frequented by *John Ruskin* who persuaded the owner to rent him a room and then another one for one of his friends. The English author, who apparently wrote most of *The Stones of Venice* there, is largely responsible for giving this little hotel its start.

▲▲**Seguso** Map II D-2 (Lines 1 or 2: Accademia; 5 or 8:

Zattere). Zattere 779, tel. 52-22-340; 36 rooms on the Rio S. Vio near the Calcina bridge.

▲**Alla Salute "Da Cici"** Map II D-3 (Line 1: Salute), Fondamenta Ca'Balà 222, tel. 52-35-404. 50 rooms. Remarkably well situated: a short walk to the north and you reach the end of the Grand Canal at the church of *S. Maria della Salute*, a short walk to the south and you discover the Canal of *La Giudecca*.

▲**Casa di Stefani** Map III E-1 (Line 1: Rezzonico), Calle Traghetto S. Barnaba 2786, tel. 52-23-337. 11 rooms. A small pensione in a quiet district where students outnumber the tourists.

▲**Doni** Map III D-6 (Lines 1, 2 or 4: S. Zaccaria), S. Zaccaria 4656, tel. 52-24-267. 11 rooms. Situated behind the basilica of San Marco, near the Riva degli Schiavoni.

▲**Wildner** Map III E-6 (Lines 1, 2 or 4: S. Zaccaria), Riva degli Schiavoni 4161, tel. 52-27-463. 20 rooms. Close to the *Danieli*, on the quay which faces *S. Giorgio Maggiore*.

Hotels on the Lido
(most close Oct. 15 to March 15).

▲▲▲▲**Excelsior Palace** Map p. 146 D-1 (April to Oct.), Lungomare Marconi 41, tel. 52-760-201, telex 410023. 245 rooms, air cond., gardens, tennis, beach with tents/cabins. A hotel of world renown with the best site on the beach, close to the Casino which is one of four in Italy, and to the *Palazzo del cinema* (August film festival): a seaside resort in itself.

▲▲▲**Des Bains** Map p. 146 B-3 (May to Oct). Lungomare Marconi 17, tel. 765-921, telex 410142. 270 rooms, air cond., swimming pool, tennis. Although it is situated at the junction of the broad *Gran Viale S. Maria Elisabetta* and the beach front, it is a pleasant, quiet hotel because of the large, beautiful gardens which surround it and shield it from the traffic. The film *Death in Venice* was shot in this hotel. Just across the road is the beach with its private cabins and huts reserved for the use of the hotel clients.

▲▲**Cappelli's** Map p. 146 B-2 Gran Viale 41 tel. 52-60-140. 104 rooms, air cond.

▲▲**Biasutti** Map p. 146 B-2 Via Dandolo 29, tel. 52-60-120, telex 410666. 72 rooms.

▲▲**Centrale** Map p. 146 B-2 Via M. Bragadin 30, tel. 52-60-052. 38 rooms.

▲▲**Helvetia** Map p. 146 B-2 Gran Viale 4, tel. 52-60-105. 54 rooms.

▲▲**Quattro Fontane** Map p. 146 C-1 Via Quattro Fontane 16 (55 yards/50 m from the *motoscafi* Casino station), tel. 768-814. 72 rooms, tennis, gardens, quiet.

▲▲**Villa Mabapa** Map p. 146 A-3 Riviera S. Nicolò 16, tel. 52-60-590. 29 rooms.

▲▲**Villa Otello** Map p. 146 B-2 Via Lepanto 12, tel. 52-60-048. 34 rooms, popular with touring students.

▬ FOOD IN VENICE

You will find, as in every tourist center, examples of the very best and of the very worst food (do you need to be reminded that prices are high?), but Venice is crammed with good restaurants, *trattorias* (cheaper) and steak-houses, as well as bakeries and pastry shops that can be very appealing. If you are in a hurry, *tavola caldas* that go back to the days before self-service was invented, offer a very wide range of cold or hot dishes; bakeries sell delicious cakes and a variety of loaves; and there is, of course, no shortage of *pizzerias*.

Prices follow a very simple rule: the closer a restaurant is to San Marco and the other leading tourist attractions, the higher its prices will be. The same "tourist menu" with identical pasta, main dish and ice cream could be almost double the price near the basilica as in less visited areas. In addition, the peacefulness and the attractiveness of the surroundings, as well as the courtesy of the waiters, will increase – generally speaking – as the price decreases. Do not forget that the prices shown on the menu may not include service or cover charge (*coperto*) which can turn out to be quite arbitrary.

Venetian cooking is essentially based on the produce of the sea and the lagoon, but the quality of the rice (*riso*), pasta, ham (*prosciutto San Daniele*, more renowned than Parma ham), calf's liver (*fegato*) and, in season, mushrooms (*funghi*) is quite remarkable. As for sea-food, we suggest: *granseole*, small sea spiders from Yugoslavia, served well cooked and cold with a seasoning of olive oil and lemon; *moleche* (pronounced mo-aykay), small swimming crabs, gathered during the molting season and grilled (the new soft shell and pincers, can also be eaten); *seppie in teci*, cuttlefish served with *polenta; baccalà mantecato*, salt cod garnished with anchovy and cinnamon. Burbot (*ruspo*), John Dory (*San Pietro*), sea-perch (*branzino*) and eel (*bisato*) are very nicely prepared.

Rice is served either as a *risotto* (often with seafood) or cooked in chicken broth with green peas (*risi e pisi*). There is a great variety of pasta; we recommend in particular the green pasta, and the thick black spaghetti (*bigoli in salsa*) which is served with an anchovy sauce. Venetians serve up their pasta and risotto as an appetizer – if you fancy a *risotto* and you don't want to lose your appetite for the main course, ask for a *risottino* (a small *risotto*). Pasta with large red beans makes an excellent soup (*pasta e fagioli*) but the most famous dish is undeniably calf's liver (*fegato alla veneziana*) cooked in thin slices with onions; it is truly excellent as long as the onions don't overwhelm the dish.

Cold spinach is currently served with most dishes. Do not overlook the *scampi* and the *canoce* (types of crayfish).

Cheeses are excellent, the most original without doubt being fresh *mozzarella* served with black olives and a seasoning of olive oil and herbs, especially marjoram – which, however, does not come from Venice.

The local beer is light and of a high quality. The wines of Venezia are very pleasant: among the reds, you should select the *Valpolicella*, the *Bardolino*, or the *Merlot*; among the whites, try the *Soave*, the *Prosecco*, the *Gambellara*, the *Tocai*, the *Collio*, etc.

If you don't want to drink alcohol, ask for still or sparkling mineral water because, in Venice, tap water is heavily chlorinated; tea suffers from it, but coffee can easily cope with it. If you like sparkling water, ask for a bottle of *San Pellegrino* or *Recoaro*; if you prefer still, choose *Fiuggi*. *Ferrallele* water is somewhere between.

Restaurants

Venice

From 60,000 lire

Antico Martini, Map III E-3 (Lines 1: S. M. del Giglio; or 1, 2 or 4: S. Marco), Campo S. Fantin 1983, tel. 52-24-121. Open April to October. Closed Mondays. Elegant dinner spot (dancing after 10 pm at the nearby night club). Close to *La Fenice*, it has first-class service and decor and its menu is varied. We recommend: fillets of sole *Martini*, the *cannelloni* and the *Casanova* beef fillet because good red meat is fairly hard to find in Venice.

Cortile, Map III E-3 (Lines 1, 2 or 4: S. Marco), Calle Larga XXII Marzo 2399, tel. 708-377. Refreshing, calm atmosphere in a 14th-century courtyard. One of the two wells still supplies water and a tree with nets protects you from the pigeons; an awning can be lowered in case of rain. The chef offers quality cuisine and wines, with a special dish for each day of the week – *risotto* and veal sweetbreads with a browned butter sauce might be the Thursday special for instance, with Sunday being the day for mussel and cockle soup followed by small fried fish from the Adriatic.

Harry's Bar, Map III E-F-4 (Lines 1, 2 or 4: S. Marco), Calle Vallaresso 1323, tel. 52-36-797. Closed Mondays in the off-season. Situated in front of the motorboat jetties, it is the center of Venetian social life, as well as being one of the city's best restaurants. *Harry's Bar* was opened in 1931 by Mr Cipriani with the help of an American named Harry; it is now managed by Mr Cipriani Junior, christened Harry. Its fame spread across the Atlantic after Hemingway dined there. Any celebrity passing through Venice drops in even if only for a drink: its cocktails are excellent, especially the "Bellini" which consists of champagne and peach juice. We would recommend the green pasta, the *taglierini gratinée*, all the *risotti* (but especially the *primavera*), the *scampi carlina*, the *ravioli alla quardi*, the fillets of sole *alla Casanova* and a rather extraordinary special dish, the *Carpaccio*: slices of raw beef cut as thin as San Daniele ham, served with an aromatic mayonnaise – if you like steak tartare you will love it! Hot toast and butter appear on your table as soon as you have decided on your menu. The restaurant also has one of the best cellars in Venice.

La Caravella, Map III E-3 (same address and directions as for *Cortile*), in the old residence of Doge Pisani, tel. 708-901. Closed Wednesdays. A quiet, distinguished restaurant with some remarkable dishes: lobster soup, *bigoli* (morsels of bread with soup) with anchovy and onions, Christopher Columbus pancakes, fillet of raw beef *alla Tiziano*, etc.

La Mansarde, Map III E-3 (Lines 1: S. M. del Giglio or 1, 2 or 4: S. Marco), Campo S. Fantin 1917, tel. 710-455. Open evenings only, "club style": inquire from the manager of the restaurant *Al Teatro* who will direct you to the 3rd floor. There you will find, indoors or on the terrace, a dinner-dance in the best Venetian tradition (orchestra).

40,000-60,000 lire

Al Colombo, Map III D-3 (Lines 1, 2 or 4: Rialto), Corte del Teatro 4619, near Campo S. Luca, tel. 52-22-627. Closed Thursdays. A spacious, pleasant decor with modern paintings; a magnificent *hors d'œuvre* display greets you on arrival; you can select equally good meat or fish, but the calf's liver *alla Veneziana* is especially worth recommending.

Al Giglio, Map III E-3 (Line 1: S. M. del Giglio), Campo S. M. del Giglio 2477, tel. 89-456. Closed Wednesdays; open from February to November. Another good, comfortable restaurant with a good table. There is a terrace on the square next to *Haig's Bar* and the *Ala* hotel.

Al Graspo de Uva, Map III C-4 (Lines 1, 2 or 4: Rialto), Calle dei Bombuseri 5093 tel. 52-236-47, in a little *calle* near the bridge. Closed Mondays and Tuesdays. This typical restaurant, very secluded although close to one of the busiest bridges in Venice, is appreciated by know-ledgeable Venetians. The owner buys his supplies daily and has the reputation of insisting on freshness.

Alla Colomba, Map III E-4 (Lines 1, 2 or 4: S. Marco, or 1: S. M. del Giglio), Piscina de Frezzeria 1665, tel. 52-23-817. Open from May to October. Closed Wednesdays. This restaurant, popular with tourists, is also famous for its fine collection of modern paintings. It is recommended as an unusual spot not to be missed when visiting the City of the Doges. Not far from *La Fenice*, it has no fewer than seven dining-rooms as well as a terrace with an attractive green awning. You should try the fish with *risotto* or in buttered paper (*cartoccio Colomba*), or the famous soup with pasta and red beans (*pasta e fagioli*) which used to cause Deana, the late owner of *Alla Colomba*, to claim: "coi fagioli pago i quadri" ("I pay for paintings with beans"). Actually, it was by encouraging and feeding artists that he was able to put together the magnificent collection you can now admire in this establishment. In addition to the works of Italian contemporary artists (De Chirico, Carra Guildi, Gentelini) there is a very fine Chagall, possibly the finest in all Italy.

Antico Pignolo, Map III D-5 (Lines 1, 2 or 4: S. Zaccaria or S. Marco), Calle degli Specchieri 451, tel. 28-123. Closed Tuesdays and January. A new *trattoria* with the warm decor of a country inn and an outdoor dining area under a magnificent green awning. A very good pizzeria with excellent service. The light *zuppa inglese*, a famous dessert, is an enjoyable finish to a meal.

Da Nane Mora, Map III C-4 (Lines 1, 2 or 4: Rialto), S. Giovanni Crisostomo 5864, tel. 52-24-626. Closed Wednesdays from October to March. A very good and pleasant restaurant famous for its fillets of John Dory. If you start with a *risotto*, choose the seafood version.

Noemi, Map III D-4 (Lines 1, 2 or 4: S. Marco), Calle dei Fabbri 909, tel. 52-25-238. Closed Sunday nights and Mondays. Situated next to an ironsmith, this restaurant, which is very clean and with excellent service, is one of the gastronomic meeting-places of Venice. To start, you can choose soup, *hors d'œuvre* or pasta: we recommend as an appetizer the *antipasto alla Noemi* made with prawns, crayfish and octopus in a special sauce; for soup, try the fish soup or, if you prefer, the bean and pasta soup; among the pasta dishes, one of the best is the *cannelloni alla Nonno Piero*, with spinach, chicken and baked cheese. The fish are very fresh and might be served fried, like the *grigliata alla Noemi*, or baked like the *filletto do sogliola alla Casanova*, sole served with a white wine sauce with mushrooms and shellfish. The cuttlefish, *seppie in teci con polenta*, is especially good. There are two wines which deserve special mention: a white, the *Malvasia Collio*, and a red *Cabernet, Grave del Friuli.*

Peoceto Risorto, Map III B-3 (Lines 1, 2 or 4: Rialto), Calle Donzella 249, tel. 52-25-953. Closed Mondays. Situated fairly close to the fish market, this is a friendly little restaurant which specializes in fried fish. You could start with the *granseole*, tiny sea spiders from the Yugoslav coast that are so well cooked and seasoned you can eat them shell and all.

Poste Vecie, Map III B-3 (Lines 1, 2 or 4: Rialto; or 1: S. Silvestro), Pescherie 1608, tel. 52-23-822. Closed Tuesdays. Located behind the fish market, the *Pescheria*, it specializes in fish dishes. The extent of the menu and the quality of the cooking will meet all your requirements.

Taverna La Fenice, Map III E-3, (Line 1: S. M. del Giglio; 1, 2 or 4: S. Marco), Campiello La Fenice 1938, tel. 52-23-856. Closed Wednesdays. Another good, stylish restaurant near the theater, frequented by musicians and actors, in a quiet setting of greenery and water.

Trattoria do Forni, Map III D-5 (Lines 1, 2 or 4: S. Zaccaria or S. Marco), Calle degli Specchieri 468 and Calle della Guerra, tel. 52-32-148. A well-patronized restaurant specializing in Venetian cooking in a comfortable and lively atmophere, with the option, in summer, of eating outdoors.

20,000-40,000 lire

Al Teatro, Map III E-3 (Lines 1: S. M. del Giglio; or 1, 2 or 4: S. Marco), Campo S. Fantin 1917, tel. 52-21-052. Closed Mondays. The meeting place of anyone involved with *La Fenice*, whether actors, directors or spectators. A lively bistro-café (newspaper stand, tobacco) open till 1 am. On fine days, tables are set up in the square. Good yeast bread.

Alla Madonna, Map III C-2 (Lines 1: S. Silvestro; or 1, 2 or 4: Rialto), S. Polo 594, tel. 52-23-824. Closed Wednesdays. An amazing range of seafood set out on a long table awaits you at the entrance. One of the best fish restaurants; great activity at lunchtime and quick and efficient service. The choice is wide: try the *moleche* (soft-shelled crabs) and the cuttlefish with *polenta*.

Alla Rivetta, Map III 1-3 (Line 1: S. Silvestro), Campiello dei Meloni 1479, tel. 52-24-246. This very simple little restaurant is situated on a main traffic artery between the Campo S. Polo and Campo S. Aponal, but it is set back far enough that you can still enjoy the charming *Rio dei Meloni*.

Antica Locanda Montin, Map II D-2 (Line 1 or 2: Accademia; 5 and 8: Zattere), Fondamenta Eremite 1147, tel. 52-23-307. This *trattoria*, in a delightful setting, is frequented by artists and intellectuals. There are a number of modern paintings on the walls. Lunch or dinner is served in a very pleasant garden, weather permitting.

Trattoria Al Vagon, Map III B-4 (Lines 1, 2 or 4: Rialto), Sottoportego del Magazen 5597, tel. 52-37-558. A very pleasant *trattoria* situated only a few yards away from the major traffic area leading from S. Marco to the station and the *Piazzale Roma*. You can eat outdoors on the bank of the *Rio dei SS. Apostoli*.

The islands and the Lido

At the Lido:

20,000-40,000 lire

Belvedere, Map p. 146 B-2 opposite the S. M. Elisabetta landing stage, tel. 52-60-115. Closed Mondays. Quality restaurant and snack bar.

Da Ciccio, Map p. 146 C-1 Via Sandro Gallo 241, Lido, tel. 52-765-489. Closed Tuesdays and November. Excellent.

Da Valentino, Map p. 146 C-1 Via Sandro Gallo 81, Lido, tel. 52-60-128. Closed Mondays and November. A wide open chimney divides – or links – the dining room and the kitchen. Do try the charcoal-broiled fish and, in season, small fried cuttlefish. Also take the opportunity to taste the *Trenette all'astice* (spaghetti with lobster) and the shellfish *risotto* cooked in sea-water.

Il Porticciolo, between the Lido and Malamocco, tel. 52-768-384. Specializes in fish from the lagoon.

Trattoria da Scarso, opposite the Alberoni-Lido jetty, tel. 765-834. Popular fashionàble restaurant. A local literary prize is announced there each year.

Murano:

Ai Frati, Fond. Venier 4, tel. 736-694, *trattoria* specializes in seafood.

Burano:

30,000-50,000 lire

Ai Pescatori, Via Baldassare Galuppi, tel. 730-605. Closed Mondays. A good Burano restaurant which is beginning to enjoy a sound reputation.

Da Romano, Via Baldassare Galuppi, tel. 730-030. Closed Mondays. A *trattoria* with a wide-ranging menu and excellent cuisine. It is one of the best restaurants in the lagoon, decorated with a collection of paintings like some of the other Venice restaurants. Among the best dishes are fried or poached fish (eel, John Dory, tail of turbot, sole, sardines); small fried fish; fish soup; *risotto* with fish or cuttlefish or, more simply, spaghetti in butter *al dente*: very lightly cooked, the pasta keeps its firm texture.

S. Pietro in Volta:

20,000-40,000 lire

Da Memo, on the Pellestrina sea front, tel. 688-125. Recommended for seafood.

Da Nane, on the Pellestrina shore which continues the line of the Lido beyond the Malamocco narrows, tel. 688-110. The special dish is the *pasticcio di pesce* (lasagne stuffed with fish) but, one way or another, you will find yourself dining on fish or other seafood.

Torcello:

Around 60,000 lire

Locanda Cipriani, tel. 730-757. Open from March 19 to November 10. Closed Tuesdays. Six "tourist" menus from *Harry's Bar* for people in a hurry and a special menu for others who may choose to dine in a rustic-style (but modern) dining-room, on a large veranda, or in a quiet flower-filled garden. The pasta stuffed with meat or fish is particularly good as are the *risotto*, the *gnocchi*, the fish from the lagoon and shellfish. For lunch reservations tel. above or 52-36-797 (*Harry's Bar*). A *motoscafo* will pick you up in front of the *Danieli* hotel at midday to reach Torcello 35 min. later. It leaves at 3 pm, and you arrive back in Venice at 3.40 pm.

40,000-60,000 lire

Il Ponte del Diavolo, tel. 730-401. Between the landing stage and the cathedral.

Cafés

Florian Map III E-4-5 (Lines 1, 2 or 4: S. Marco or S. Zaccaria), Piazza S. Marco. The most famous café in Venice: this establishment, opened by Floriano Francesconi in 1720 as *Venice Triumphant*, soon became known by its owner's name: people went to *Florian's*. It is closely associated with the history of Venice, not only because of the celebrities who frequented it (one could hardly list them all), but also because of the writers who described it and the artists who painted it: a famous canvas by *Bertini* (1721-1793) shows *Guardi*, the follower of *Canaletto*, offering his paintings to *Florian's* customers. In short, one could hardly pass through Venice without going to *Florian's* for a coffee. Afternoon tea means a tempting trolley of cakes but you can get memorable sandwiches at any time. The doors that open onto the gallery are decorated with marble and paneling; inside you may admire the salon of the seasons, the hall of portraits, and the little Chinese and Senate salons decorated in 1900. The atmosphere is warm and rich because of the walnut woodwork and the cherry red velvet seats. At the back, alcohol-lovers will find a bar which is hard to beat. Bear in mind that prices are higher when the orchestra is playing.

Quadri Map III E-4-5 (Lines 1, 2 or 4: S. Marco or S. Zaccaria), Piazza S. Marco. The other café on St Mark's Square with numerous tables outside. (One word of advice: don't sit in the first row of the gallery because of the pigeons – they're fed grain by helpful tourists which can make them "over-productive"!) Wise customers choose the terrace of the *Quadri* for the sun and the *Florian* for the shade: your decision should be dictated by the season. Two open-air orchestras play Viennese waltzes or recent tunes; *Vivaldi* would be more appropriate. Again, prices are higher when the musicians play.

Chióggia Map III E-5 (Lines 1, 2 or 4: S. Zaccaria or S. Marco), Piazzetta S. Marco. The special merit of this café (the decor is a pale modern version of the *Florian*) is that it faces the Palace of the Doges. You will be able to admire that Gothic masterpiece with an appropriate feeling of serenity – especially if your feet hurt!

Al Todaro Map III E-5 (Lines 1, 2 or 4: S. Marco or S. Zaccaria), at the angle of the Piazzetta and the quay; one of the best locations for a café, where the greatest number of gondolas and motorboats are moored. You can rest while admiring this unique man-made waterscape, with the church of *S. Giorgio Maggiore* as a background. Excellent ice cream.

Ice Cream

Paolin Map III E-2 (Lines 1 and 2: Accademia), Campo S. Stefano 2962. Have an *espresso* or a *cappuccino* but ice cream is the favorite at any time of the year.

Gelateria Causin Map II C-2 (Line 1: Ca' Rezzonico), Campo S. Margherita. a little shop, easy to miss, but one of the few ice cream specialists of Venice.

Cucciolo, Aldo, Nico Map II D-2 (Line 5: Zattere). Three ice cream shops selling a fine range of their products on the jetties along the *Zattere* near the *Gesuati* church. Customers find it hard to pass up the *gianduiotto*, a chocolate ice cream bar dipped in frozen whipped cream.

Titta on the Lido, Via Maria Elisabetta, is one of the best ice cream makers in Venice.

Coffee Shops

Goppion Map III D-4 (Lines 1, 2 or 4: S. Zaccaria or S. Marco), Merceria. Situated in one of the busiest commercial streets in Venice, this coffee-roasting establishment offers one of the best cups of coffee you can taste. You can also take a few packets of coffee away with you.

Bottega del Caffè Map III D-6 (Lines 1, 2 or 4: S. Zaccaria), at the angle of Calle delle Rasse and Salizzada S. Provolo, between S. Marco and S. Zaccaria. A coffee shop we recommend as strongly as the previous one, but a little off the main pedestrian thoroughfares. High quality coffee to drink there or take away.

Wine Bars

Al Milion Map III C-4 (Lines 1, 2 or 4: Rialto), Corte del Milion 1. This renowned *baccaro*, situated where Marco Polo's house once stood, serves wines of good quality with snacks and a typically Venetian buffet. A highly recommended spot.

Fiaschetteria Toscana Map III C-4 (Lines 1, 2 or 4: Rialto), S. Giovanni Crisostomo. This establishment offers fine local wines with grilled suckling pig and a wide range of fish *hors d'œuvres*.

Tavola Calda

These are self-service restaurants which provide varied and plentiful cold or hot dishes. Quick and good.

Al Teatro Goldoni, Map III D-4 (Lines 1, 2 or 4: Rialto), S. Marco, Ponte del Lovo 4747.

Au Chat qui Rit, Map III E-4 (Lines 1, 2 or 4: S. Marco), Calle Frezzeria 1133. Closed Fridays.

Bakeries (*panetterie*)

Il Fornaio Map III D-4 (Lines 1, 2 or 4: Rialto), Calle S. Luca 4759, just by the Campo S. Luca. This bread shop is one of the sights of Venice, so great is its range of loaves large and small; all types of fresh pasta are also on sale.

Milani Map III E-4 (Lines 1, 2 or 4: S. Marco), Calle Frezzeria (the street which leads on from Calle Vallaresso beginning in front of the S. Marco landing stage). There is a very wide choice of loaves, buns and pastries, particularly tarts. Close by in the same street, you will find something to go with a snack: the **Baldan** delicatessen, one of the best in Venice, the locals claim, for Parma and San Daniele ham.

Pastry Shops (*pasticcerie*)

These are not tearooms.

Marchini Map III E-2 (Line 1: S. M. del Giglio), Calle del

Spezier 2769, just by the Campo S. Stefano. A wide choice of cakes; we especially recommend the light rice cake.

Vio Map III B-1 (Line 1: Riva di Biasio), Rio Marin 890. Closed on Wednesdays.

Rosa Salva Map III D-4 (Lines 1, 2 or 4: S. Marco or S. Zaccaria), Calle Fiubera 951. Closed on Fridays.

Rosa Salva Map III D-4 (Lines, 1, 2 or 4: Rialto), Merceria S. Salvador 5020. Closed on Sundays.

PRACTICAL INFORMATION

Opening Hours of Museums and Public Buildings

In Venice, timetables are irregular, unpredictable and often whimsical. Official opening hours are more or less adhered to in museums, apart from strikes, repairs and other events controlled by mysterious forces. As for churches – the ways of the Lord are impenetrable... We have attempted to give you details that are as accurate as they can be, but without guarantees. Don't lose heart: follow the advice we give you, and, in all likelihood, you will succeed. On arrival, start by getting the latest timetables from the Tourist Office (*see p. 73*). Then, if you want to see a particular work of art, telephone beforehand for the most up-to-date information on opening hours (*Accademia, Correr, Rezzonico,* etc). Finally, take some 100 lire coins with you to operate the lighting systems on church paintings, as well as a mirror (some places hire them out) so that Tintoretto and Tiepolo, those kings of the painted ceilings, don't give you a crick in the neck. A word of warning about one misinterpretation which has confounded more than one tourist: *giorno festivo* is not a special visiting day. It means "holiday", in other words..closed; *giorno feriale* is the indication that the museum is open.

Post and Telephone Services

The main Post Office is situated in the *Fondaco dei Tedeschi*, just by the *Rialto* bridge (Map III C-4; Lines 1, 2 or 4: Rialto). When you go to buy some stamps you will have the opportunity of visiting one of Venice's finest buildings. The international phone service, which, in Italy, is separate from the postal service, is by the exit of the *Fondaco* and is open 24 hours a day.

SHOPPING IN VENICE

In Venice you will find everything you could find in a major city: the latest fashions, shoes, leather goods, hats, jewelry. The great houses of Paris, Milan, Rome, Florence and London all have outlets there but you should first seek out the local manufacturers, visit the shops of glass- and lace-makers: there are some in every district, but we have selected a few which we feel are particularly worthy of recommendation. We have listed not only specialist shops but also other boutiques to assist you in your shopping expeditions. In every field, quality is our prime consideration.

Lace and Linen

Jesurum Map III D-5 (Lines 1, 2 or 4: S. Zaccaria or S. Marco), Ponte Canonica 4310, behind the basilica. This extraordinary shop, situated in the old *Scuola S. Apollonia* is a real historical building which suggests the ancient splendor of the great trading companies. Here you can buy, or merely admire, the finest lace (in Italian, *merletti*) as well as the most beautiful house linen and the loveliest women's fashions, especially beachwear. You will also see beautifully set and decorated tables. *Jesurum* is a name associated with the history of Venetian lace-making. *Michelangelo Jesurum*, an energetic businessman (and a friend of the noted politician *Paolo Fambri*), promoted the rebirth of the lace industry after the decline of the Most Serene Republic. He set up a lace factory in this very building although a large number of women outworkers lived in *Burano*. Venice's lace industry goes back to 1597, thanks to the Doge's wife, *Morosina Morosini Grimaldi*, who was very fond of lace; she had set up a workshop for lace "and other curiosities" at *S. Fosca*, employing 130 women. Intended originally for church apparel, lace appeared in time on bodices and dresses, then on men's clothes, on fans, bed linen, curtains and even on footwear.

Tradition relates an interesting tale. One day a sailor gave his girl a strange marine plant, a *Halynedia opuntia*, popularly known as "siren's lace"; after he had sailed away, she endeavored to reproduce its peculiarities in needlework and thus was born the famous "Venetian point". Recently, the lace industry has been going through difficult times, which is why *Jesurum* now includes beach and summerwear among its products, as well as household linen.

Glassware

Venetian glass owes its worldwide reputation to the fact that it has remained a craft; it is still made by individual artisans. Furthermore, artists who are related to the few families of *Murano* glassmakers create the designs, and the glassmakers have wisely decided to limit strictly the number of pieces they turn out of any one model. Consequently, other glassware firms outside Venice have not been able to dislodge it from its position as a world leader in glassware production.

Generally speaking, you don't have to go to Murano to buy glassware: the major producers all have retail outlets and display centers, often located in *palazzi* that provide a magnificent setting for these works of art. (*See Antique Dealers*).

Pauly Map III D-5 (Lines 1,2 or 4: S. Zaccaria or S. Marco), Ponte Consorzi (cross the Piazzetta dei Leonici at the left of the basilica and take the first bridge on the left). Three floors of period chandeliers and mirrors, engraved glassware, antiques, table settings, 1930s vases.

Salviati Map III F-3 (Line 1: Salute), Calle del Bastion 195 along the Grand Canal. Splendid exhibition in an appropriate setting.

Venini Map III D-5 (Lines 1, 2 or 4: S. Zaccaria or S. Marco), S. Marco 314 to the left of the basilica. New creations each year. Specializes in contemporary lighting.

Vistosi Map III F-2 (Lines 1, 2 or 4: Accademia), display-room at S. Vio 886; the shop is near Campo S. Luca, Calle del Teatro 4609 (Map III D-4; Lines 1, 2 or 4: Rialto).

L'Isola Map III E-4 (Lines 1, 2 or 4: S. Marco), Campo S. Moisè 1468. A very stylish new shop, specializing in design glassware, especially for the table. These are items made in Venice following the authentic processes of the lagoon's glassmakers, both in the workmanship and the color, but in line with modern taste. This first attempt to renew the forms of Venetian glassware is a great artistic success.

Amadi Bruno Map III D-2 (Line 1: S. Tomà), Calle dei Saoneri 2747. Amadi is a young artist who works in the shop and specializes in miniature items: ants, spiders, cherries, molluscs so small you almost need a magnifying glass to see all the amazing details. The beautifully finished work is in excellent taste which is, by no means, a universal quality. Superb little gifts for a few thousand lire.

Clothing

The garment industry seems to be turning increasingly towards mass production or the more extreme styles. Here are a few fairly classical shops for the "middle of the road" buyer.

Roberta di Camerino Map III E-4 (Lines 1, 2 or 4: S. Marco), Calle Larga dell'Ascensione 1255; also at the Lido, Lungomare Marconi 32/a. (M & W) Italian *haute couture*, as well as handbags, shoes, luggage, accessories.

Luisa Spagnoli Map III D-4 (Lines 1, 2 or 4: S. Marco or S. Zaccaria), Merceria S. Zulian. (W). Renowned for its woolens and knitwear.

Gegia Bronzini Map III E-4 (Lines 1, 2 or 4: S. Marco or S. Zaccaria), in the S. Marco arcade, Café Quadri side. (W). A range fairly similar to Luisa Spagnoli's.

Camiceria S. Marco Map III E-4 (Lines 1, 2 or 4: S. Marco) (M & W) Calle Vallaresso, 1340. Specializes in blouses, shirts, and pajamas made to measure, with an almost endless choice of materials.

Elite Map III D-5 (Lines 1, 2 or 4: S. Marco or S. Zaccaria) (M) Calle S. Marco, 284. English chic with fine Italian fabrics for suits, shirts and sweaters.

Rovoletto Map III D-5 (Lines 1, 2 or 4: S. Marco or S. Zaccaria) Merceria dell 'Orologio. Specializes in ties.

And now for the more spectacular *alta moda* (high fashion):

Rossella Map III D-4 (Lines 1, 2 or 4: Rialto) (W) Calle del Teatro, 4600. Laura Biagotti and Krizia designs.

Elisabetta alla Fenice Map III E-3 (Line 1: S. Maria del Giglio) (W) Campo del Teatro (opposite *La Fenice*). Valentino, Ferré designs.

Alta Moda Map III E-4 (Lines 1, 2 or 4: S. Marco) (W) Calle Vallaresso, 1318. Valentino, Parisini, Senegale designs.

Fendi Map III E-4 (Lines 1, 2 or 4: S. Marco) (W) Calle Vallaresso, 1312. Couture fashion.

Missoni Map III E-4 (Lines 1, 2 or 4: S. Marco) (M & W) same address. De luxe knitwear.

Venetian Shop Map III D-6 (Lines 1, 2 or 4: S. Zaccaria) (W) corner of Campo S. Filippo. The latest fashions, along with more reasonably priced models.

La Coupole Map III E-3 (Lines 1, 2 or 4: S. Marco) (M & W) Calle Larga XXII Marzo. Leather fashions, Enrico Coveri, Montana.

Volpe This chain of shops which specializes in informal men's and women's wear has three branches in Venice: S. Aponal, 1228 (Map III C-3, Line 1: S. Silvestro); S. Bartolomeo, 5257 (Map III C-4, Lines 1, 2 or 4: Rialto); Frezzeria, 1286 (Map III E-4, Lines 1, 2 or 4: S. Marco).

Leather Goods

La Bottega Veneta Map III E-4 (Lines 1, 2 or 4: S. Marco) (W) Calle Vallaresso, 1337. Original and elegant creations; also exclusive silk scarves.

Vogini Map III E-4 (Lines 1, 2 or 4: S. Marco) (M & W) corner of Calle Vallaresso and Calle Larga XXII Marzo. More classic styles. Luggage.

Carlo Daniele Map III D-5 (Lines 1, 2 or 4: S. Zaccaria or S. Marco). Calle Specchieri, 449. This beltmaker has a wide range of buckles and can quickly make a belt of your choice to fit, in leather or any other material. A small family firm, efficient and with reasonable prices.

Shoes

Fratelli Rossetti (M & W). Two addresses for this high-class shoe specialist: Salizzada S. Moisè, 1477 (Map III E-4; Line 1, 2 or 4: S. Marco) and Merceria S. Salvador, 4800 (Map III D-4; Line 1, 2 or 4: Rialto).

Magli e Bruno Magli (M & W). Two addresses also for a good choice of attractive, fashionable shoes: Calle Frezzeria, 1696, and Calle Vallaresso, 1302 (Map III E-4; Lines 1, 2 or 4: S. Marco).

Varese Map III E-4 (Lines 1, 2 or 4: S. Marco) (M & W) on the Orseolo basin opposite the hotel *Cavalletto*. Good quality shoe shop with a good range.

Santini e Dominici Map III E-3 (Line 1: S. Maria del Giglio) (M & W) Calle Larga XXII Marzo, 2967. A shoe specialist with a colorful and youthful range.

Morile Bozzi Map III B-3 (Line 1: Ca' d'Oro), Strada Nuova, 3822/a. The *alta moda* of men's and women's footwear. Colorful styles with some eccentric models.

Gloves

Galvan Map III D-5 (Lines 1, 2 or 4: S. Zaccaria or S. Marco) Merceria dell' Orologio, 229. A wide range of high quality gloves for men and women.

Ladies' Lingerie

Cima Map III D-4 (Lines 1, 2 or 4: Rialto), Merceria del Capitello, 4918. Articles in pure silk.

Fabrics

Valli Map III D-4 (Lines 1, 2 or 4: Rialto, S. Marco or S. Zaccaria) Merceria S. Zulian. All types of Italian fabrics sold by the metre; high fashion printed silks and exclusive embroidered and sequined articles.

Jewelry, Gold- and Silverware

Missiaglia Map III D-5 (Lines 1, 2 or 4: S. Marco or S. Zaccaria) Piazza S. Marco, next to the *Quadri*. Luxury items on a par with what you would find in the best London or Paris jewelers, as well as exclusive creations by Venetian artists (necklaces, lighters).

Nardi Map III D-5 (Lines 1, 2 or 4: S. Marco or S. Zaccaria) Piazza S. Marco, next to the *Florian*. The other great jeweler of Venice offers some very fine crafted items in hard stone, as well as small clocks, boxes, frames, powder boxes and a special line, the *Otellos* (black heads set with precious stones).

Antique Dealers

If you are in no hurry and you like antiques, you will find several well-stocked antique shops on or near the Campo S. Maurizio (Map III E-2-3; Line 1: S. Maria del Giglio). Don't be too hopeful of discovering great bargains...

Beppe Patitucci, Campiello della Feltrina, 2511/b. Bronzes, textiles.

La Bottega d'Arte, Campiello della Feltrina, 2513/a. Ancient vases, paintings, etc.

Paolo Zancopè, Campo S. Maurizio. Antique dealers since 1838 specializing in 16th-18th century Venetian glass, unusual items (retorts, telescopes), paintings, engravings.

Modern Painting and Sculpture

Ravagan Art Gallery Map III E-5 (Lines 1, 2 or 4: S. Zaccaria or S. Marco) Piazza S. Marco 50/a: among other things, exhibits and sells limited editions of De Luigi horse sculptures as a kind of tribute to the horses of S. Marco.

Galleria Il Capricorno Map III E-4 (Lines 1, 2 or 4: S. Marco) Piscina di Frezzeria, close to *La Fenice*. If you are in search of modern paintings, you will get the best advice here.

Il Traghetto Map III E-3 (Line 1: S. Maria del Giglio) Campo S. Maria Zobenigo, 2460. This unusual and friendly little gallery is the only one exhibiting nothing but the work of Venetian artists all year round.

Ceramics

La Bottega d'Arte Martini Map III E-3 (Line 1: S. Maria del Giglio), S. Maria del Giglio, 2459, offers stoneware and rustic pottery, lampbases, and old engravings on Venetian themes attractively framed.

Bogo Map III C-5 (Line 5: Fondamenta Nuove) opposite the hospital, Campo SS. Giovanni e Paolo. A craftswoman who works in front of you, firing plates and utensils with your name on them.

San Sebastiano Map III C-D-1 (Line 1: Rezzonico), opposite the Scuola dei Carmini. A young potter who reproduces various decorative patterns of ancient Venice on tiles, dishes, plates, and other items.

Rigattieri Map III E-2 (Line 1: S. Angelo) Calle dei Frari, 3532/36, between Campi S. Stefano and S. Angelo. A large choice of merchandise, from a soup tureen in the shape of a hen, to decorative eggs. All items for sale are from the small town of Bassano in the countryside behind Venice.

Al Canale Map III C-4 (Lines 1, 2 or 4: Rialto) Ruga Rialto, 973. Just a few steps from the Rialto, a superb collection of ceramic jewelry. Magnificent colors, very reasonable prices starting at a few thousand lire.

Stationery

Legatoria Piazzesi Map III E-3 (Line 1: S. Maria del Giglio) Campiello della Feltrina (near Campo S. Maurizio). A book binder who sells original binding paper, games of snakes and ladders, card games, tarot decks, and all sorts of boxes covered with original silk-screen designs.

Paolo Orbi Map III D-3 (Line 1: S. Angelo) Calle della Mandola, 3653. Paper, photo albums and sketch pads.

Masks

Carnival masks are one of the most typical souvenirs you can take home from Venice. Rather than going into ordinary shops, which can offer you only a limited range and whose profit margin is often considerable, we suggest three highly reliable specialists. You will have the opportunity to follow the various stages of manufacture and experience the atmosphere which surrounds this time-honored craft.

Balocoloc Map III B-2 (Line 1: S. Stae) Calle del Scaleter, 2235. Here you will find the classic *bauta* and other traditional masks, as well as tricorne hats and veils that recall the paintings of Pietro Longhi.

Clanetti Map III C-6 (Lines 1, 2 or 4: S. Zaccaria, or 5: Fondamenta Nuove) Barbaria delle Tole, 6657. Near Casanova's last home, G. Clanetti runs a creative workshop. In addition to classic carnival masks, he has a whole range of human and animal heads.

Mondonovo Map II D-2 (Line 1: Rezzonico) Rio Terà Canal, 3063. Venetian artist Giano Lovato has a world-wide reputation: in addition to his output of traditional items, he supplies many theater groups and takes part in festivals. His workshop, close to the Campo S. Margherita is worth a detour. Lots of imagination and fantasy, and some very affordable prices.

▬ SOME USEFUL ADDRESSES

Banks

In theory, they are open Monday to Friday from 8.30 am to 1.30 pm and from 2.45 to 3.45 pm.

American Express Map III E-4 (Lines 1, 2 or 4: S. Marco) S. Moisè, 1471, tel. 700-844.

Banca d'America e d'Italia Map III E-4 (Lines 1, 2 or 4: S. Marco) Calle Larga XXII Marzo, 2216, tel. 700-766. Visa cards.

Banca di Napoli Map III E-4 (Lines 1, 2 or 4: S. Marco), Campo S. Gallo 1112, tel. 52-31-700.

Banca di Roma Map III D-5 (Lines 1, 2 or 4: S. Zaccaria or S. Marco) Mercerie dell'Orologio, 191, tel. 26-796.

Consulates

Great Britain, Cancelleria, Dorsoduro, 1051, tel. 27-207.

United States, the U.S. consulate is located in Trieste. Via Roma 9, 4th floor. (40) 68-72-89.

Useful Telephone Numbers

Police Rescue Service (*Polizia Soccorso Publico*): 113

Medical Help (*Pronto Soccorso*): 52-30-000

Fire Brigade (*Vigili del Fuoco*): 52-22-222

Tourist Information

To find out the opening hours of museums and other buildings, to get a map of Venice, or, if necessary, a hotel room, inquire at the *Azienda Autonoma Soggiorno Turismo* which works in association with the *Ente Provinciale del Turismo* (Regional Tourist Office). There are four offices:
– at the station (Stazione S. Lucia), tel. 715-016.
– at the Piazzale Roma, tel. 52-27-402.
– just behind St Mark's Square, Calle Larga Ascensione, 71/c, tel. 26-356.
– at the Lido, Gran Viale, tel. 765-721.

Theaters

Teatro La Fenice Map III E-3 (Line 1: S. Maria del Giglio) S. Fantin, 2549, tel. 52-23-954

Teatro del Ridotto Map III E-4 (Lines 1, 2 or 4: S. Marco) Calle Vallaresso, tel. 52-22-939

Teatro Goldoni Map III D-4 (Lines 1, 2 or 4: Rialto) Calle del Teatro, tel. 52-707-583

The Grand Canal, 2⅓ miles/3.8 km in length, wends its way through Venice. It carries the heaviest water traffic in the city: launches, motorboats, gondolas, light and heavy barges and, of course, festival traffic.

ITINERARY A
THE GRAND CANAL

The Grand Canal owes its fame to the *palazzi* that line it: their varied styles meet all the artistic criteria of this great waterway, 98 to 230 ft (30 to 70 m) wide, in which their facades are reflected. Its winding course adds an element of warm intimacy which makes it unique in the world. Probably even more than St Mark's Square, it is the symbolic image of Venice.

In this section you will find a list of the main palaces and buildings which deserve particular notice (the most outstanding are marked with stars) as your *vaporetto* takes you from the Piazzale Roma or the railway station to the San Marco landing stage opposite the Dogana di Mare. Buildings open to visitors are described in other tours, as they are easily accessible on foot. The journey of just under 2½ miles/4 km will take you 40 minutes by *accelerato* Line 1 or 28 minutes by *diretto* Line 4 (June to September).

The boat may well be slow, but it still goes too fast for you to admire both sides of the canal because the palaces are so tightly packed together. Indeed, the only reference points you can use are three bridges and sixteen landing stages or motorboat stops which you will, of course, find mentioned in the following pages. One solution is to make the journey twice (once in each direction). At night the Canal takes on a new appearance: palaces emerge from the shadows, while lights, mirrored in the water, create an unforgettable atmosphere. Some 170 years ago you might have come across Lord Byron, whose habit it was to float on his back, smoking a cigar and holding up a lantern to avoid being hit by the oar of a passing boatman!

To get a better idea of the fabulous artistic wealth of the palaces, bear in mind, as you go down the Grand Canal, that their facades used to be covered with frescoes, providing a rich backdrop for the daily life of the inhabitants. Sadly, most have faded away.

"The finest street I believe to be found anywhere in the world," wrote the French chronicler Commynes in the 15th century. The Grand Canal today, is still Venice's main traffic artery, plied by the *traghetti* and boats

Left Bank

FERROVIA STOP (S. Lucia Station)
Church degli Scalzi.

Bridge of the Scalzi (1934).

Church of S. Geremia (1760).
Opening of the *Cannaregio canal* at the corner of the *Palazzo Labia* (17th-18th century).
Church of S. Marcuola.

S. MARCUOLA STOP

★**Palazzo Vendramin-Calergi,** completed by Lombardo in 1509, one of the finest *palazzi* along the Grand Canal. Wagner died here in 1883. It is now the *Winter Casino* (open October 1 to April 1).
Palazzo Erizzo (15th century).
Palazzo Gussoni, by Sanmicheli (16th century).
Palazzo Fontana (16th century).
★**Ca' d'Oro** (The Golden House), the finest Venetian Gothic palace (1440). It is the home of the *Franchetti Gallery.*

CA' D'ORO STOP

Palazzo Sagredo (Gothic).
Palazzo Michiel dalle Colonne (*Ca' Matteoti*, 17th century).
Ca' da Mosto (13th century Venezo-Byzantine). Beautiful windows.
Palazzo Bolani (late 16th century).
★★**Fondaco dei Tedeschi** (main Post Office), the old German traders' warehouse of the 12th-14th centuries, restored by Scarpagnino in 1506.

★**Rialto Bridge,** single arched, 157 ft/48 m long, 72 ft/22 m wide, with three rows of stairs plus shops, built from 1588 to 1592 by *A. da Ponte.*
RIALTO STOP
Palazzo Dolfin-Manin, by Sansovino, 1550.
Palazzo Bembo (Gothic).
Palazzi Farsetti and *Loredan* (Town Hall) with 12th- and 13th-century facades.
★**Palazzo Corner Martinengo** (17th century), home of the Venice Tourist Office.

ferrying people and goods; an artery, in every sense of the word, which nourishes the pulsating heart of the City of the Doges.

Right Bank

S. CHIARA STOP
(Piazzale Roma)
Papadopoli Gardens.
Church of S. Simeone Piccolo.

Bridge of the Scalzi (1934).

RIVA DI BIASIO STOP

★Fondàco dei Turchi, (13th century) Venezo-Byzantine *palazzo*, marble facade with double gallery (*Museum of Natural History*).
Former grain stores of the Republic, in brick.
Palazzo Belloni-Battagià, by Longhena (17th century).
Palazzo Tron (1590).

S. STAE STOP
Church of S. Stae, Baroque facade.
Palazzo Foscarini (16th century).

★Palazzo Pesaro, a masterpiece by Longhena, the finest Baroque palace in Venice (1679-1710), home of the *Gallery of Modern Art* and the *Oriental Museum.*
Palazzo Corner della Regina, by Domenico Rossi (1724).
Palazzo Brandolin (Gothic).
Pescheria, fish market.
Fabbriche Nuove del Rialto, by Sansovino (1552-1555).
Erberia, fruit and vegetable market.
Fabbriche Vecchie di Rialto, by Scarpagnino (16th century), site of the law-courts.
Palazzo dei Camerlenghi, by Bergamasco (1528).

★Rialto Bridge
S. SILVESTRO STOP

Palazzo Businello, (restored in the 18th century). Byzantine decorations.
Palazzo Papadopoli (16th century) built in the Sansovino style (restored).
Palazzo della Madonnetta (12th-13th centuries).
Palazzo Bernardo, Gothic (1442).

Facing one of the three bridges which cross the Grand Canal, the church of the Scalzi possesses one of the finest Baroque facades in Venice, with two tiers of twinned columns and statues attributed to B. Falcone.

The city first took shape in the early 9th century on the islands known as the Rialto, a name which has become a synonym for the heart of Venice.

Left Bank

★**Palazzo Grimani** (Appeals Court) by Sanmicheli (1556-1572).
Palazzo Cavalli (15th century) Gothic windows.
Palazzo Tron, Gothic (15th century).
Palazzo Volpi, (Renaissance).
★**Palazzo Corner Spinelli,** by Mauro Codussi (15th-early 16th century) has an austere elegance.

S. ANGELO STOP

Palazzo Mocenigo, made up of four buildings (16th to 18th century), where Lord Byron stayed in 1818.
Palazzo Contarini delle Figure, Renaissance building attributed to Scarpagnino (1504).
Palazzo Moro-Lin (17th century).
★**Palazzo Grassi** or **Cini** (1735) by Massari. Grand staircase decorated with 18th-century frescoes. Headquarters of the *International Art Center*.
Church of S. Samuele, Romanesque campanile (12th century).

S. SAMUELE STOP
(launches)

Ca' del Duca (begun in 15th century, unfinished).
Palazzo Giustinian-Lolin (17th century) by Longhena.

Accademia Bridge
Palazzo Cavalli-Franchetti, (15th-century Gothic, restored 19th century).
Two *Palazzi Barbaro* (one 15th-century Gothic, the other 17th century).
★**Palazzo Corner** or **Ca' Grande** (Prefecture), a fine building by Sansovino (1537).

S. MARIA DEL GIGLIO (ZOBENIGO) STOP

Palazzo Gritti (15th century). The most famous hotel in Venice.
Palazzo Fini, by Tremignon (1688).
Palazzo Contarini-Fasan (15th-century Gothic).
Palazzo Giustinian (15th-century Gothic). City Tourist Office.

S. MARCO STOP

Right Bank

Palazzo Grimani, by the Lombardi (early 16th century).
★Palazzo Pisani, (15th-century Gothic).
Palazzo Tiepolo-Valier, in two buildings (15th-16th centuries).
Palazzo Giustinian-Persico (16th century).

S. TOMA-FRARI STOP

Palazzo Grimani (17th century)
★Palazzo Balbi, with a fine 1590 facade, on the bend of the canal.
Rio Foscari (used by the *motoscafi* on their way to the Piazzale Roma).
★Ca' Foscari (15th century Gothic). Advanced Institute of Commerce.
Two *Giustinian palazzi* (one 15th century, the other 17th century).
★Ca' Rezzonico, begun by B. Longhena, completed by Massari. Home of the museum of the 18th century.

REZZONICO STOP

Palazzo Loredan (15th century).
Palazzo Contarini degli Scrigni, made up of two buildings: one built by Scamozzi in 1609, the other in 15th-century ogival style.
Galleries of the Accademia.
ACCADEMIA STOP

Accademia Bridge
Palazzo Manzoni-Angaran (Renaissance).
Palazzo Loredan (16th century).
Palazzo da Mula (15th century).
Palazzo Venier also known as *Palazzo dei Leoni* begun in 1749, but construction stopped upon completion of the ground floor; home of the Peggy Guggenheim collection.
Palazzo Dario (1487), attributed to P. Lombardo.
Abbey of S. Gregorio (14th century).

S. MARIA DELLA SALUTE STOP

★★Church of S. Maria della Salute.
Punta della Salute and *Dogana di Mare* (Customs house, 17th century), surmounted by a *statue of Fortune*, between the Grand Canal and the *Canale della Giudecca*.

Venice's beauty has grown over the centuries, even though its size has not. The Campanile, 320 ft/98 m high, thrusts skywards the golden angel poised on its spire, while the Palace of the Doges opens its arcades onto the Piazzetta.

ITINERARY B
THE HEART OF VENICE

This second itinerary covers only a short distance but it takes in so many buildings, works of art and places of interest (including two cafés, the *Florian* and the *Quadri*) that a detailed visit would require several days. To plan your visit, bear in mind that the basilica and, to a lesser extent, the *Palazzo Ducale* (Palace of the Doges), draw very large crowds. You would be well advised, especially during high season, to go there early in the morning. For instance, get to the basilica at around 9.30 am, go to the *Marciano* museum at 10 am and from there, go on directly to the palace. The Correr and the other smaller museums are less crowded and can be visited in comfort at any time.

▬ ST MARK'S SQUARE

Piazza San Marco★★ (Map III E-4-5. Lines 1, 2 or 4: S. Marco or S. Zaccaria). 574 ft (175 m) in length. This monumental "square" has been the heart of the city since the earliest days. Occupying the site of the gardens of S. Zaccaria's convent, it was laid out in the second half of the 12th century and first paved with bricks set out in a herringbone pattern. The present paving dates from 1723. It was designed by the architect *Andrea Tirali*, and consists of Emilian flagstones and Istrian white stones forming sets of decorative bands. It is a work of art which reflects patterns used for carpets at that time.

The *Piazza*, bound by the splendid buildings of the Procuratie, the clock tower and the basilica, is one of the grandest places in the world. It was the setting of sumptuous festivals in the 17th and 18th centuries and, each year, on the Feast of the Ascension, a great arts and crafts fair which lasted several days was held here.

These lively scenes, recorded in their day by Guardi and Canaletto, have their modern counterparts around the three cafés in the *Piazza*, especially at *Florian* where, in 1899, *Marcel Proust*, accompanied by his mother and his close friend Marie Nordlinger, enthused over its Louis-Philippe decor.

The "new" and the "old" *Procuratie*, built over galleries lined with shops and cafés, give the square its architectural uniqueness. The building on the north side of the square, which extends from the clock tower, is called the **Old Procuratie** (*Procuratie Vecchie*) and dates from the 16th century. Built in the Venezo-Byzantine style of the earlier *palazzi* (12th century), it contains 50 arcades over a length of 498 ft (152 m). It was originally built by Mauro Codussi but was restored, after a fire, by Bartolomeo Bon and Guglielmo Bergamasco. It was the residence of the Procurators, the highest officials of the time, who controlled the property of the basilica.

Across from the Old Procuratie are the **New Procuratie** (*Procuratie Nuovè*), the work of Vincenzo Scamozzi and Baldassare Longhena. Built in the 17th century, there is a gallery of 40 arcades, and the facade is remarkable for its two levels of high windows between columns in the three Greek orders (Corinthian, Doric, Ionic) which create a perfect classical harmony.

At the back of the square, the **Fabbrica Nuova** (the New Factory) owes its existence to Napoleon, who had it built on the site of the church of S. Gimignano (16th century) in order to complete the classical balance of the Piazza. This "Napoleon wing", (architects: Giovanni Antolini and Giusepe Soli, 1810), also built over a gallery, has only one level and is based on the architectural style of the *Procuratie Nuove* but the facade is topped by statues of 14 Roman emperors (sculptors: Bosa and Banti). The statue of Napoleon which formed the central feature has been taken down. You enter the Museo Correr from this building (*see end of the itinerary*).

The Clock Tower

Built at the end of the 15th century on a plan by Mauro Codussi, the **Torre dell'Orologia** (Map III D-5) is a typical Renaissance structure. The central edifice overlooking the *Mercerie* Gate contains the clock (decorated with signs of the zodiac) and is topped by a terrace above which a large bell hangs. Two statues (sculpted by Paolo Savin and mechanically operated) strike the bell on the hour. They are known as the *Mori* (the Moors) because of the dark hue of the bronze they are made from. The clock has no face or hands but two rectangular frames – one on either side of a Madonna with Child – display the time, rather like a modern digital watch: hours on the left, minutes on the right. These frames also form doorways through which an angel and the Three Wise Men come out to pay homage to the Virgin every hour during Ascension Week. The whole is dominated by a winged lion, the symbol of St. Mark.

The two symmetrical structures on each side of the tower are the work of Pietro Lombardo (1506). Two levels were added by Giorgio Massari in 1775. You can reach the terrace and observe the complex mechanism of the clock through a door on the left of No. 147 Merceria dell'Orologio. (*Open 9 am – 12 noon and 3 – 5 pm; Sundays and holidays 9 am – 12 noon. Closed Mondays*).

According to a legend recorded by Leone Dogo, it took Paoli

Rainieri and his son Carlo three years to perfect the clock mechanism. It is claimed that, when they had finished, the Senate ordered them to be blinded so that no other city would have such a clock.

THE BASILICA OF SAN MARCO★★★

The basilica (Map III D-E-5), designed by an unknown architect, was erected in the second half of the 11th century. There were two earlier buildings, one built during the 9th century when the body of St Mark was transported to Venice from Alexandria in Egypt (in 828), the other after the first burned down during the 10th century.

The present basilica is the very symbol of Venice's history with its rich decorations. Not a square inch remains free of mosaic or marble and it is adorned with a breathtaking mixture of works of art of different periods and origins. Many of these masterpieces came from the East at the time of the Crusades, which has led certain critics to comment that S. Marco is the result of systematic pillaging. The church you admire today was enriched as it evolved over the centuries, reflecting a feverish and unbounded trading activity. Consequently, some people see it as the most beautiful building in the world, while others are startled by this assemblage of ill-assorted elements.

Be that as it may, the *Chiesa d'Oro*, the Golden Church, retains the structure which its architect planned for it before the gold and marble began to cover it inside and out. Inspired by the Church of the Holy Apostles in Constantinople (now gone), it is a Byzantine edifice in the shape of a Greek cross, with five cupolas. Its dimensions are: length (including the narthex) 253 ft/76.5 m, width 170 ft/52 m at the facade, 205 ft/62.6 m at the transept.

The basilica opens at sunrise for religious offices, but the treasury, the *Pala d'Oro* and the Marciano Museum have more restricted hours (*see below*). In addition, as the basilica has been undergoing substantial restoration work over recent years, there is always the possibility that some of the items we refer to may be temporarily covered up.

The Exterior of the Basilica

The *facade*, with its two levels of five arched sections, has retained its early Byzantine appearance in spite of a Gothic crowning (15th century) by Dalle Masegne and the Lamberti. This is the finest Gothic stonework ensemble to be found anywhere in Italy. Below the line of arcades decorated with 17th-century mosaics which are not in keeping with the ensemble (from left to right: *Deposition, Descent from the*

The Basilica of San Marco, the very symbol of Venice's glory, has gradually *been covered in precious marbles, but the structure of the early Byzantine facade, with its five entrances and its five upper portals, remains unaltered.*

Cross, Resurrection, Ascension), you can see a long terrace where the Doge stood with the senators and visiting dignitaries to watch the celebrations in the square below. Above the central portal, four handsome copies of the famous **Horses of San Marco** "seem to prance and neigh", as Petrarch once wrote. The originals are inside (*see Marciano Museum*). Also note the fine overhanging gargoyles in the Tuscan style, installed during the 15th century.

The lower level, with its five deep-arched portals leading to the narthex, is also decorated with mosaics. From right to left: *Removal of the Body of St Mark from Alexandria, Arrival of the Body in Venice, The Last Judgement* (all three from the 17th century), *Homage to the Saint's Body* (18th century), and *Translation of the Saint's Remains to the Church of S. Marco* (13th century) in which the basilica is shown in its original state.

The **central portal,** flanked by four marble columns, consists of three concentric arches decorated with allegorical bas-reliefs (months, virtues, trades) of the 13th – 14th centuries. Notice, especially, the sculptures by unknown artists depicting the life of Venetian workers: *squeraroli* (boat-builders), *mureri* (masons), *calegheri* (shoemakers), *pescatori* (fishermen). The bronze doors are 11th century Byzantine; between the arches note six fine Oriental bas-reliefs, examples of Early Christian art.

Detail of the Byzantine facade of San Marco: the saints, carved by sculptors from Tuscany and Lombardy, seem about to fly off into space.

The **San Alipio portal,** on the left, was the first to be built and deserves special attention. The superb mosaics of the tympanum are unique specimens of late 13th-century art and the decorations above the portal complete a composition of truly Oriental splendor. The delicacy of this work is reminiscent of a miniature or of embossed leather.

Before you enter the basilica, look overhead in the **narthex.** The *mosaics* of this atrium are as astonishing as they are varied. The older ones are more naive and narrative and could even be called comic strips. In the upper section (13th century) among the biblical scenes, the *Drunken Noah* will bring a smile to most lips. Above the main door, view *The Ecstasy of St Mark* (17th century) from a cartoon by Titian and don't miss *The Virgin and Saints* (11th century) in the alcoves or, across the vault, *The Last Judgement* (16th century) from cartoons by Tintoretto. Lower your eyes. The *paving* (11th – 12th centuries) which stretches out before you includes three slabs of red marble: they mark the spot where the Emperor Frederick Barbarossa made peace with Pope Alexander III in 1177.

The splendor of the main facade should not cause you to overlook the two lateral facades where you can admire the richness and the variety of the marble. The sight is truly rewarding, and you will not regret spending a few moments tracing the intricate labyrinths of colored marble.

The Interior of the Basilica

Now, at last, the time has come to step into the basilica. You stand there startled by the most astonishing profusion of embellishments to be seen anywhere. In this softly-lit sanctuary, a silence reigns which is due, in part, to astonishment and the sense of wonder felt by all those who enter this magic place: "Whoever penetrates for the first time into the golden atmosphere of the basilica gains the impression of having stepped into the fabulous Orient. The "Roman" solemnity of the surroundings is diminished by the light streaming from the cupola windows onto the mosaics, illuminating them, flickering over the lamps, and gleaming on the marble flagstones. The anonymous architect of S. Marco conceived it as a Greek cross with a large central nave, a raised sanctuary over the crypt and a polygonal apse. Heavy pillars and elegant columns, mostly in the Byzantine style, mark off the smaller naves and support the upper galleries. Five arched hemispheric domes are situated over each arm of the cross and at the center; 4783 sq yds/4000 sq m of mosaics cover the walls and the cupolas, and a kind of marble carpet, begun in the 12th century, spreads out beneath the feet of the visitor. A colored marble iconostasis separates the sanctuary from the rest of the church and is surmounted by a fine 14th-century group by Jacobello and Pier Paolo dalle Masegne. Beyond, you can glimpse the magnificent altarpiece, the *Pala d'Oro*, a masterpiece of the Venetian goldsmith's art..." (Rodolfo Pallucchini).

The floor (dating from the 12th century) was very uneven but is now stabilized after extensive injections of reinforced concrete. It looks like a gigantic Oriental carpet, while the walls of the nave, brilliantly capitalizing on the natural features of the marble, resemble enormous tapestries. The decorators have created works of art in which the forms link the natural with the creative.

Jumbled booty. Contrasted with the facade, the interior decor of the basilica appears well-balanced but, studied in detail, the various elements that go towards creating that whole emerge as a kind of golden calf, the loot of pillaging soldiers or the purchases of merchants keen to show off their wealth. These works of art were displayed with great skill and Venetian artists drew their inspiration from them until the time came, in the 15th century, when a truly Venetian style began to develop. Before taking you, step by step, to view the works of art of the basilica, we urge you to cast a last admiring glance at the **marble pillars** – more than 500 of them – veined and resplendent like so many gigantic precious stones. Those of the baldachin are so well polished that they seem to be made of ivory.

Let us look first at the *tympanum of the middle portal* which is decorated with a 13th-century mosaic (partly restored): *Christ, the Virgin and St Mark*, a remarkable work in the Byzantine style. Look then at the *cupolas* of the Pentecost and the Ascension. The first of these, the oldest, is decorated with an extraordinary mosaic (*Pentecost*, 12th century) depicting the Holy Spirit coming down over the Apostles in the form of tongues of fire; on the next arch note the *Scenes of the Passion* (Byzantine style, 12th century).

The second central dome, the *Ascension*, is covered with an early 13th-century mosaic. Strongly influenced by Byzantium, it already shows signs of a burgeoning Venetian style. Completed by the *Virtues* (between the windows), the *Evangelists* and the *Four Rivers of the Bible* (in the pendentives), this decoration is further enriched by four Romanesque angels in gilded wood placed at the base of the arches.

The *Battistero* (temporarily closed) contains the baptismal font based on designs by J. Sansovino (1545). There is a bronze cover decorated with bas-reliefs (*Life of St John the Baptist*) and topped with a statue of the saint (1570). The *tombs of Doges Andrea Dandolo* and *Giovanni Soranzo* (14th century) are also here. The vaulted ceiling is covered with a mosaic (14th century) depicting scenes from the childhood and life of Christ. The baptistery links with the *Zeno* Chapel, named after a cardinal buried there. The commemorative monument is by A. Lombardo; above, is a late 13th-century mosaic (restored).

The raised sanctuary, over the crypt, is separated from the nave by an iconostasis surmounted by 14 statues by Dalle Masegne (1394) and a silver and bronze cross (14th century).

La Pala d'Oro★★★ (*Open 9.30 am – 4.30 pm; Sundays and holidays 2 – 4.30 pm*). Above the *main altar*, under which lies the body of St Mark, a ciborium is held up by **four alabaster columns** with 12th-century capitals. Behind the altar stands the sumptuous gold reredos (ornamental screen), the *Pala d'Oro*, which includes pieces dating from the 5th to the 13th centuries. It is one of the finest and largest (11½ ft × 4½ ft/3.48 m × 1.40 m) examples of the goldsmith's art: over 80 figured enamels are framed in precious stones. The upper section is decorated with seven enamels depicting the major feasts of the Church. The large panel is built around a central motif – Christ giving his blessing, surrounded by the Evangelists – with, overhead, the image of the Virgin with Doge Falier and the Empress Irene at her side; the surrounding enamels depict angels, apostles and prophets.

The **Treasury** (*same opening hours as the Pala d'Oro*). If the great *Pala d'Oro* attracts you, you will not be able to resist visiting the Treasury, where a vast number of objects which were brought back from Constantinople in 1204 are kept. In the sanctuary, to the left, there is an altar with an Eastern *alabaster reredos*; in the alcoves, there are 110 reliquaries. Above the central alcove of the vestibule, in a tabernacle, is the *Reliquary of the Blood of Christ* in gold and jasper with 11th-century Byzantine enameling. In the room on the right, numerous precious items date back to the 10th century (chalices, cups, reliquaries). Other points of interest in the room include the throne of St Mark, a reliquary in the form of a seat from the 6th or 7th century; icons, bindings of holy books, candelabra, glass cups, caskets, an urn dating back to 414 BC and a late 12th-century altar frontal. The finest piece, in a display case in the center of the Treasury Room, is, without doubt, the *Ortophoron*, an 11th or 12th-century silver casket for holding holy wafers.

Marciano Museum

Open daily 10 am – 4.30 pm.

If you go up the stairs to the right of the central portal in the narthex, you will reach the small Marciano Museum and galleries. From here, you can admire the interior of the basilica and see the mosaics at close quarters, and also emerge onto the terrace between the hooves of the four horses.

The museum contains fragments not only of mosaics, a polyptych by Paolo Veneziano and Persian carpets of the 15th century, made of silk with gold and silver threads, but also the original horses of S. Marco. These remarkable statues look as though they are made of copper but they are really of gilded bronze; they were brought from Constantinople in 1204, where they adorned the Hippodrome towers. No one has been able to determine with any precision the origin of these Graeco-Alexandrine or Roman masterpieces (2nd, 3rd, possibly 4th century AD). Napoleon so admired them in 1797 that he had them sent to Paris where, for 18 years, they graced the Arc de Triomphe of the Carrousel. Their existence might have ended tragically had a decision not been made to protect them from pollution, they having been affected by damp, salt and sulfur dioxide. They were carefully restored and replaced by the four copies which now stand outside.

The Campanile of San Marco★★

Open daily 10 am – 7.30 pm. Elevator to the upper section.

The present building dates back to 1912; the original campanile collapsed on July 14, 1902, fortunately without injuring anyone. Until then, it had stood perfectly straight, which goes to show that the noticeable list on many other Venetian campaniles is not necessarily a sign of their impending collapse. The S. Marco campanile was the oldest structure on the square, work on it having begun at the end of the 9th century. The poor quality of some of the materials used, a fire in 1489, and water seepage, all contributed to its sudden collapse despite maintenance and restoration work already carried out on it. It is 324 ft/98.6 m high, and its characteristic silhouette owes much to the Romanesque style of the base and the Renaissance decorations of the upper section; its elegance is completed by a harmonious pattern of colors: the red of the bricks, the white of the Istrian stone, the green of the oxidized copper sheeting on the pyramidal roof and the gilt of the statue of the angel dominating the structure. The plinth between the belltower and the roof is decorated on each of the four sides with high relief representations of Justice and the Lion.

We urge you to go up to the upper platform to enjoy an aerial view of the various districts and buildings of the city. Better still, if the weather is clear you will discover not just the Adriatic beyond the Lido, but the lower Alps and even the Alps themselves including *St Mark's Peak*.

La Loggetta★★

Sansovino's delightful little building opposite the *Porta della Carta*, nestling against the foot of the campanile, harmonizes

The Molo facade of the Palace of the Doges, completed in 1404 when the great central balcony with pillars, niches and spires, was finished. It was the work of the Dalle Masegne brothers.

perfectly with the neighboring library which he also built. The marble Loggetta was built in 1540 to house the guards during sessions of the Grand Council. Rebuilt after the collapse of the campanile with its original stones, and more recently restored with the help of the London Foundation, the *Loggetta* reflects the traditional form of Roman triumphal arches. In the niches, four superb bronze statues by Sansovino represent Peace, Apollo, Mercury and Minerva (1540).

▬ THE PALACE OF THE DOGES★★★

Open daily 8.30 am $-$ 7 pm during the summer season, 9 am $-$ 4 pm during the rest of the year. To be quite sure, ring 52-24-951. The itinerary suggested may be affected by restoration work in progress in various rooms.

The **Palazzo Ducale** is one of the finest Gothic buildings anywhere in Europe. It goes back to the 9th century, when it was already the seat of government but, at that time, it was probably no more than a turreted castle. Successive rebuildings have resulted in the splendid edifice of the present day which was probably never conceived as a whole. The south facade must have been finished around 1404 with the completion of the great central pillared balcony, niches and spires, the work of the Dalle Masegne brothers. Next, work was carried out on the Piazzetta side. Running counter to all the laws of traditional construction, openings are predominant along the lower section, with the arcades of the portico and the aerial effect of the *loggia*, while the upper section consists of a long wall of pink and white marble forming a regular geometrical pattern. This reversal of traditional design is no whim; it follows the rule of Venice: a rhythmic interplay of light and shade. The spaces of the lower section suggest solidity, the pink wall gives the impression of merging with the light. The beautiful gallery resting on the 18 arcades of the portico, is 246 ft (75 m) long on the quay side, while on the Piazzetta (17 arcades) it is 234 ft (71.5 m) long.

The solid *columns* of the portico have various decorated capitals, the bases now being some 16 in./40 cm below pavement level as a result of slow subsidence. The groups at the corners and the *capital* design follow a symbolic and didactic pattern related to the life of Man and Nature. To see them more effectively, begin with the *Molo* side which is largely 14th century in style. It reflects the methods of Venetian sculptors and Lombard master craftsmen at a time when the northern influence was strong. Then look at the 15th-century examples of flamboyant Gothic, and continue on to the *Judgement of Solomon* by Pietro Lamberti at the angle near the *Porta della Carta*, attributed to Giovanni and Bartolomeo Bon. Notice, along the same facade, the ninth column of the gallery from the left: it is supported by *two pillars of red Verona marble*. It was here that death sentences were announced. From the Molo, at the end of the facade, you will see the wing of the palace which runs along the *Rio di Palazzo*. Built between 1483 and 1498, it is the work of the great Renaissance sculptor and architect Antonio Rizzo. This masterly composition, balanced and vigorous, emphasizes the relationship between light and shade.

The Bridge of Sighs* (*Ponte dei Sospiri*) is really an enclosed passageway linking the Palace of the Doges with the prisons. Built in the 17th century of white Istrian stone by a little-known architect, Antonio di Bernardino, it owes its name to the fact that it led to the offices of the State Inquisitors where prisoners were sentenced. When they saw the S. Marco basin through the bridge's small windows for the last time they let out, so it is said, pathetic sighs...

To enter the Palace, go through the *Porta della Carta* situated to the left of the basilica's Treasury. Before you go in, however, note on your left, in the angle formed by the wall, a strange porphyry group, the Tetrarchs (or *Mori*, because whenever a figure seemed a little dark-skinned, it was referred to as a Moor), a Syrian or Egyptian work of the 4th century representing, legend tells us, four Saracens turned to stone for trying to steal the S. Marco treasure. Others identify them as the Roman emperors Diocletian, Maximinus, Valerianus and Constantine. The decorations of the reliefs and the marble are of an exceptional richness.

La Porta della Carta* (the Gate of Notices, so named because official announcements were posted there), very recently restored by the British Committee, is once again revealed in its original polychrome splendor. It is the most elaborate example of Venetian flamboyant Gothic art. The work of G. and B. Bon (1443), it is decorated above the architrave by a remarkable statue of Doge Foscari kneeling before the lion of Saint Mark; in the niches stand statues of Strength and Prudence (below) and Hope and Charity (above).

You enter the courtyard through the Foscari arch, decorated with bronze replicas of Adam and Eve by Rizzo (the famous originals are in the palace). Three buildings flank this courtyard; the eastern one dates from the Renaissance (its facade runs along the *Rio di Palazzo*), the other two, south and west, are a mixture of Renaissance and Gothic styles because they were rebuilt in the 16th century after a fire in 1483. Against the sky you will see elegant Gothic white marble adornments reminiscent in style of the celebrated lace made by the women of *Burano*.

The Giants' Staircase★ (*Scala dei Giganti*) gets its name from two colossal (but mediocre) statues by Jacopo Sansovino. The Doge went up these stairs after his election to receive his ducal cap on the upper landing. The **Scala d'Oro** (golden staircase) then gives access to a succession of rooms leading to the Doge's apartments; completed in 1559, probably from plans by Sansovino, the staircase was adorned by Alessandro Vittoria with white and gold.

In each of the rooms you will find works of art that deserve your attention. In the *vestibule*, note the ceiling painting by Tintoretto, *Justice and Peace Offering the Scales and the Sword to the Doge*. In the *Room of the Four Doors*, ceiling frescoes are by Tintoretto and, on the wall, you can see *Doge Grimani Adoring Faith*, painted in part by Titian. In the **Room of the Anti-Collegio** (rebuilt from plans by Palladio after the 1574 fire), stucco decorations surround a small hexagonal ceiling by Veronese, restored by Ricci. You will also have the opportunity to admire one of Veronese's best paintings, **The Abduction of Europa** (1580), many times copied and reproduced and notable for the luminosity of the colors and sense of movement. If you like Tintoretto, you will be pleased to find a feast of mythological subjects before you: *Vulcan's Forge, Mercury and the Graces, Bacchus and Ariadne, Minerva Rejecting Mars*.

The Collegio Hall★, where the Doge received ambassadors, papal nuncios and noblemen returning from missions, is decorated with paintings, sculptures and a wooden dais. It is one of the finest examples of the late Renaissance style. The room is particularly noted for its great canvas by Veronese, *The Victory of Lepanto* (*c.* 1578). It shows *Sebastiano Venier*, the admiral of the Venetian fleet, thanking Christ who, surrounded by St Mark, St Justine and allegorical figures, gives him His blessing. The artist's female allegorical figures symbolize Venetian virtues. The coffered ceiling, entirely adorned with gilt sculptures, is decorated by Veronese (1577): in the center, *Allegory of Faith*; at the back, *Venice Enthroned with Justice and Peace*; above the entrance, *Mars and Neptune* with the *the Virtues* at the side. Tintoretto paintings hang on the walls, including *Doge Andrea Gritti Before the Virgin* above the doorway.

The Senate Room✶ displays all the glories of Baroque art with its ornate cornices (1581) and its paintings (1585-1595). In the middle of the ceiling, you will see Tintoretto's *Venice Receives the Gifts of the Sea*, and his *Truth* and *Eloquence* are in the corners above the throne. The other ceiling paintings are by A. Vicentino, M. Vecellio, Palma the Younger and Tintoretto (*Doge Pietro Loredan Praying to the Virgin*). Over the throne, you will see Tintoretto's *Doges Pietro Landro and Marcantonio Trevisan Adoring the Dead Christ*. Going along the sides you will arrive at the entrances to the *Antichiesetta* and the *Chiesetta* (chapel) which is decorated with stuccos and frescoes; the altar is dominated by a marble *Madonna and Child* by Sansovino.

The 10 magistrates in charge of public safety, known as the Council of Ten, held their meetings in the **Sala del Consiglio dei Dieci,** for which Veronese painted several canvases (see his *Old Oriental Man* above the dais); his *Jupiter Destroying the Vices*, taken to the Louvre in 1797, has been replaced by a copy. On the walls, under a frieze of *putti*, there are paintings by Vecellio, F. and L. Bassano, and Aliense's fine *Adoration of the Magi*.

From there, you go on to the **Armeria** to view a superb collection of armor and weapons: halberds, rapiers, daggers, arquebuses, and even a culverin.

One floor down, by the Scala dei Censori, are the Doge's private quarters (*often closed, particularly when special exhibitions are being arranged*). In one room you will see the celebrated **statues of Adam and Eve** by Antonio Rizzo, a gifted Venetian artist of the Renaissance, who was born in *Verona*.

You will now reach **the Great Council Chamber,** the largest and the most sumptuous in the Palace. The paintings have been restored by the Venice Committee. The carved and gilded wood ceiling is a true marvel, comprising paintings by some of the most famous artists of the day. From the Molo side, by the throne: Veronese's *Siege of Scutari*, Francesco Bassano's *Victory of Polesella*, Tintoretto's *Victory of Argenta* and *The Capture of Gallipoli*, Francesco Bassano's *Rout of Emperor Maximilian at Cadore*, Palma the Younger's *Capture of Padua*. In the center, going towards the dais, Palma the Younger's *Venice, Crowned by Victory, Welcomes the Pacified Provinces*, Tintoretto's *Doge Nicolo da Ponte Receiving a Crown of Laurel from Venice*, and Veronese's *Apotheosis of Venice*, notable for the subtle interplay of light and the boldness of the foreshortenings. On the courtyard side, *The Capture of Smyrna* by Veronese, *The Victory of Casalmaggiore* by Francesco Bassano, *The Victory of Riva* and *Defense of Brescia* by Tintoretto, *The Victory of Maclodio* by Francesco Bassano, *The Victory of Cremona* by Palma the Younger.

In the panel at the back, is Tintoretto's *Paradise* (1590), one of the largest canvases in the world (72 ft × 23 ft/22 m × 7 m). Helped by his son Domenico, the master took almost two years to complete it; note the incredible number of figures represented. In the cornices, there are portraits of the 76

Piazza San Marco: the Procuratie. A feeling of space dominates the lower part, with the line of arcades of the portico and the openings of the loggia creating an interplay of light and shade so typical of Venice.

Doges; that of Marino Faliero, beheaded for treason in 1355, is painted black with a brief explanation.

Below, between the windows which look out on the *Molo*, there are various *Episodes of the Fourth Crusade* painted by Vicentino, Domenico Tintoretto, Palma the Younger, Carlo Saraceni and Jean Leclerc. On the other side, Francesco Bassano, A. Vicentino, Palma the Younger, Tintoretto and others have depicted the struggle between Pope Alexander III and the Emperor Frederick Barbarossa. On the west wall, works by Giulio dal Moro, Veronese, Marco Vecellio and Aliense.

The **Sala dello Scrutinio*** (Voting Room), equally impressive in size, was restored after a fire in 1577. At the back stands the triumphal arch, which was erected by A. Gaspari in honor of Francesco Morosini. It is decorated with paintings by G. Lazzarini (1694). The ceiling has a remarkable *Conquest of Padua* by Francesco Bassano (central medallion nearest the entrance). On the wall opposite the arch hangs Palma the Younger's *Last Judgement* below a frieze by Vincentino representing the *Prophets and the Evangelists*. Other large paintings recall *The Conquests of Venice in the East* (by Vincentino, Aliense, Marco Vecellio, Tintoretto, *et al.*).

Then, returning by way of the Great Council Chamber, you can go through a series of secret passages into the prison area. The unfortunate accused often spent months or even years in these sinister cells while, only a short distance away, the happy crowds strolled in the splendid Piazza. When you cross the Bridge of Sighs, spare a thought for poor Casanova who passed this way once in circumstances far different from those of a tourist ...! If you want to know more about the darker side of the Ducal Palace, inquire about the special guided tours (*9.30, 10, 11.30 am and 12 noon; apply at the Secretariate, by the entrance*).

The visit ends at the *Hall of the Censori* after which you stroll at leisure along the balconies which look out on the *Piazzetta* and the *Molo*, as well as on the splendid interior courtyard with its two bronze-curbed wells.

▬ *THE PIAZZETTA*★★

The **Piazzetta** is a western extension of the Piazza, leading to the quay (*Il Molo*). It is bounded by the quay, the Palace of the Doges, the *Libreria Vecchia*, the *Loggetta* (at the foot of the campanile) and the basilica. The pavement is similar to the *Piazza's*. Although one of the facades of the incomparable Palace of the Doges runs along one side, it lacks the grand character of the *Piazza* but is filled with sunshine and ends at the edge of the lagoon. Here is one of the most characteristic vistas in Venice: the island of S. Giorgio Maggiore with dozens of gondolas in the foreground moored to the *pali* (piles).

There are two prominent, graceful and strong pillars of reddish Oriental granite standing on circular bases decorated with sculptures representing Venetian trades. On the pillar nearest the palace stands the glided bronze **Lion of St Mark,** possibly based on an ancient Persian chimera. On the other stands a *statue of St Theodore*, a strange mixture of classical and Renaissance elements. (St Theodore was Venice's patron saint until St Mark's bones were brought from Alexandria. The winged lion of St Mark became the symbol of Venice as its empire expanded.) Gallows used to stand between the two in the days of the Most Serene Republic and, even today, the Venetians say that walking between them brings bad luck.

The Libreria Vecchia★★

This imposing edifice was built between 1537 and 1554 by Sansovino who succeeded in designing, in the heyday of the Renaissance, a palace which harmonized perfectly with the Gothic exuberance of the Palace of the Doges.

Its beauty, and the architect's elegant solution to the problem of balancing the characteristic effects of light and shade of its noble counterpart, make this Sansovino's masterpiece. The facade includes a double row of arcades with a frieze by G. Lombardo; at the entrance, two *caryatids* (columns in the form of a female figure) by A. Vittoria. This building is the home of the Libreria Marciana and of the archaeological museum.

The Libreria Marciana (*visits by appointment, tel. 70-87-88*) was founded in 1468 by Cardinal Bessarion and is one of the largest libraries in Italy, holding half a million volumes including 3000 incunabula, and 13,000 manuscripts. It is also a museum, with illuminated manuscripts, antiphonaries, missals, gospels of the 14th century, Byzantine miniatures dating back to the 9th century, a *Divine Comedy* of the second half of the 15th century, and the famous *Grimani Breviary*, one of the most precious in all Europe with miniatures of the Flemish school (15th-16th centuries). The rooms and vestibules of the library are hung with paintings by Titian, Veronese and Tintoretto.

The Archaeological Museum (*open 9 am – 2 pm; 9 am – 1 pm Sundays and holidays. Closed Mondays*), founded in 1529, possesses a fine Graeco-Roman collection, including statues of *Aphrodite, Apollo* and *Athena*, the *Grimani Altar* dedicated to Bacchus (1st century BC), a child's head from Asia Minor, and the *Wounded Gauls* (Pergamum, 3rd-2nd century BC).

The Molo bounded by the main facade of the Palace of the Doges, the library, the Mint and the gardens of the old royal palace, is one of the most animated places in Venice. It ends in a line of steps going down to the lagoon which turns the quay itself into a work of art.

The Mint (*Zecca*), between the *Giardinetti Reali* and the *Libreria*, is another work of Sansovino's. Its massive, severe appearance is perfectly suited to its function.

▬ *MUSEO CIVICO CORRER*★★

Open 10 am – 4 pm; 9 am – 12.30 pm Sundays and holidays. Closed Tuesdays. Tel. 25-625.

Situated in the Napoleonic wing (*Fabbrica Nuova*) and partly in the *Procuratie Nuove*, the *Museo Correr* is, with the *Accademia*, one of the two great Venetian museums. It bears the name of an ardent collector, Teodoro Correr (1750-1830), scion of one of the oldest families of Venice, who left his treasures to the city. The first floor contains an outstanding historical collection and, on the second floor, there is a remarkable collection of paintings including masterpieces of the Renaissance by Antonello da Messina and Carpaccio. You are urged to spend a part of your stay in this museum which looks out on the Piazza and enables you to make a fascinating voyage to a bygone Venice.

First Floor: Historical Collection

When you have gone past the famous *Plan of Venice* by Jacopo de' Barbari (1500) which has so often been reproduced, you enter the first room in which there are works by Canova – **Daedalus and Icarus,** *Cupid and Psyche*. This great sculptor was also a gifted painter, as you can see from his *Portrait of Amadeo Svajer* (Room II). Rooms V to X are devoted to that central figure of Venetian history, the Doge: manuscripts, paintings (one by Tintoretto) depicting festivals and religious processions, numerous 17th- and 18th-century costumes, portraits of Doges. Room XI with its outstanding coin collection, is someting of a numismatist's Mecca. Room XIII is dedicated to the great naval victory of Lepanto (1571), Room XIV is dedicated to the *Bucintoro*, the famous vessel from which the Doge threw a gold ring into the water during the Wedding of the Sea ceremonials. (These symbolized the "marriage" of Venice with the sea, so important to its livelihood and power.) Rooms XVII and XVIII contain weapons. Rooms XIX to XXIII are devoted to Francesco Morosini, the last hero of the Republic who earned the city a respite when he defeated the Turks during the second half of the 17th century.

Second Floor: Picture Gallery*

The *Quadreria*, greatly enriched since the Correr legacy, traces the history of Venetian painting from its beginnings to the early 16th century. It also includes some excellent paintings from other parts of Italy and from aboard.

The first six rooms contain works from the Middle Ages. Artists were strongly influenced by Byzantium and, in the later pieces, international Gothic art. We can mention Paolo Veneziano (*The Six Saints, St John the Baptist*), Lorenzo Veneziano (*Jesus Handing the Keys of Heaven to St Peter*), Stefano Veneziano (*Madonna, St Christopher*), Stefano di Verona (*Angels With Musical Instruments*), Michele Gambono (*Madonna With Goldfinch*).

The Ferrara school is represented by Baldassare Estense's *Portrait of a Young Man* and especially by Cosimo Tura's moving **Pietà,** which reveals Flemish influences (Rooms VII and VIII). Looking at the Bartolomeo Vivarini *Madonnas* (Room VIII) we understand the part this Murano painter played during the early Renaissance in Venice. Even more important was the Sicilian Antonello da Messina who introduced the oil techniques of Van Eyck and other Flemish painters to the city: his **Pietà** is one of the finest paintings in the entire gallery; mutilations and clumsy restorations have not reduced its power.

Among the Flemish and German artists of the 15th and 16th centuries (Rooms X, XI and XII), the most important are Pieter Brueghel the Younger (*Adoration of the Magi*), Dirk Bouts (**The Nursing Virgin**) and Hugo van der Goes, whose **Crucifixion** is notable not only for its technique but also for the dramatic effect of the three figures set in a triangular composition. The

Detail of the Procuratie, St Mark's Square. The Old Procuratie, rebuilt during the first half of the 16th century, face the New Procuratie across the Square.

whole Bellini family is represented in Room XIII: Jacopo, whose acceptance of Renaissance principles at the end of his career is manifested in his *Crucifixion*; Gentile who reveals his talent as a portraitist with his *Doge Giovanni Mocenigo*; and Giovanni, with four remarkable works (*Crucifixion, Transfiguration on Mt Tabor, Pietà, Virgin and Child*). The most moving of these is probably his **Pietà** which the visitor cannot but compare with Antonello's just a short distance away.

Rooms XIV, XV and XVI concentrate on the late *Quattrocento* (15th century) and the early *Cinquecento* (16th century). Superb paintings by Marco Basaiti, Alvise Vivarini (*St Anthony*) and Lazzaro Bastiani are surpassed only by Vittore Carpaccio's *The Martyrdom of St Peter*, the enigmatic **Man in a Red Beret** and above all his **Courtesans** (*Le Due Dame Veneziane* or *Le Cortigiane*). This masterpiece owes its reputation to its pictorial excellence and also to its atmosphere of mystery. The title it is traditionally known under may well be erroneous, because critics now identify the women as members of the noble Torelli family whose coat of arms appears on a vase. Room XVII has a fine *Virgin and Child* by Lorenzo Lotto.

Rooms XVIII to XXII contain works by Greek painters, including one by El Greco, some 15th- and 16th-century ceramics, ivories and small bronze pieces.

The Museo Del Risorgimento

Same opening hours. Use your Correr admisssion ticket.

This enables you to discover a little-known period of Venetian history – the 19th century. The Austrian occupation, the Napoleonic period, the 1848 Revolution during which the Republic was briefly revived, daily life: all these are illustrated by paintings, engravings and sundry objects.

The Museo Correr also holds special exhibitions relating to the art and the history of Venice. (*Access to these is through the main entrance but a special admission ticket is required.*)

ITINERARY C
WHERE ART AND HISTORY MEET

This itinerary leads from the Piazza S. Marco to the Accademia, then to the church of S. Maria della Salute and the Dogana di Mare where the Grand Canal and the canal of La Giudecca reach the basin of S. Marco. The first section is based on the signposted walk *S. Marco-Accademia* (yellow signs) which begins at the *Salizzada S. Moisè* behind the *Museo Correr* and goes along *Calle Larga XXII Marzo*. The signs then direct you by way of the *campi* of *S. M. del Giglio*, *S. Maurizio* and *Morosini*, before reaching the *Accademia* bridge over the Grand Canal and the *Campo della Carità*, where the Fine Arts Museum (*Gallerie dell'Accademia*) is situated. This is a busy district because it is made up of numerous little streets that lead to *campi* of various sizes where you find churches and palaces. Note that some of the best shops and most of the travel agencies are situated in the *Salizzada S. Moisè*, the *Calle Vallaresso* and the *Calle Larga XXII Marzo*.

When you leave the Accademia, we suggest that you walk to the end of the Dorsoduro district by way of S. Trovaso, the Gesuati church and the Guggenheim Foundation building. On this side of the Grand Canal, everything is different: quiet, orderly, middle-class houses, an area where tourists are less numerous.

▬ FROM ST MARK'S SQUARE TO THE ACCADEMIA

The Church of S. Moisè★

Map III E-4 (Lines 1, 2 or 4: S. Marco). *Open daily 2.30 – 7 pm.*
This church, famous for its particularly elaborate facade, was built by Tremignon between 1632 and 1668. The many statues are by Meyring. Inside, you will find a Tintoretto (*Washing the Disciples' Feet*), a Pellegrini (*The Punishment of Serpents*) and a ceiling by Niccolò Bambini (*Moses's Vision*). Restoration financed by the American Committee (C.R.I.A.) began in 1967; it has recovered a wealth of paintings of the 17th and 18th centuries which now adorn the walls and altars.

The 13th-century campanile is typical of the Venetian style of the time.

Campo S. Fantin★

Map III E-3 (Lines 1: S. M. del Giglio).

Near the central section of the Calle Larga XXII Marzo, on the right, you will find the Calle Veste which leads to the Campo S. Fantin, with the church of S. Fantin and the famous *La Fenice*, the largest and most renowned theater in Venice. It often presents programs that rival those of *La Scala* in Milan. The wide range of offerings – plays, opera, comic opera, symphony concerts, chamber music – make it the Venetians' favorite center of performing arts. (*See p. 13 for more details on La Fenice*).

The interior, redecorated in 1831, is a perfect example of Baroque exuberance but is, nevertheless, in good taste. The first performances of *La Traviata* and *Rigoletto* were given here; Visconti used it for his film *Senso*.

The **Church of S. Fantin** boasts one of the finest Renaissance facades in Venice, designed by Scarpagnino and built of white Istrian stone (1549). It contains several paintings by Palma the Younger.

From Campo S. Maria del Giglio to Campo Francesco Morosini

Return to Calle Large XXII Marzo to reach Campo S. Maria Zobenigo (del Giglio).

Church of S. Maria Zobenigo, Map III E-3 (Line 1: S. M. del Giglio). *Open daily 9 – 11.30 am and 4 – 7 pm.* Renowned for its paintings by Tintoretto such as *The Four Evangelists* (1552), and for a *Madonna* attributed to Rubens. The sumptuous Baroque facade is the work of Sardi (1678-1683). The church was restored between 1970 and 1975 by the American Committee (I.F.M.). Nearby, to the right of *Campo S. Maurizio*, the *Scuola degli Albanesi* is notable for its small Lombardo facade (1531).

The **Campo Francesco Morosini,** Map III E-2 (Lines 1, 2 or 4: Accademia) is one of the city's finest *campi*. It is bounded by two superb *palazzi* and a Gothic church. The **Palazzo Loredan** (1536) has a particularly graceful Renaissance facade. On the south side, the classical **Palazzo Pisani,** which dates from the early 17th century, is built of Istrian stone and now houses the *Benedetto Marcello Music Conservatorium*. The courtyard is a fine piece of architecture. Bullfights were held in this *campo* in earlier times.

On the north side, the **Church of S. Stefano★** (14th-15th century) has a flamboyant Gothic portal, which is a creation of Bartolomeo Bon's workshop; a cloister attributed to Scarpagnino, and the most leaning campanile in all Venice, giving the impression – wrongly, we hope – that it is about to collapse. In the sacristy, there are paintings by Palma the Elder, Bartolomeo Vivarini, Paris Bordone and Tintoretto (*Washing of the Feet, Prayer in the Garden of Olives, Last Supper*).

The most logical route to follow is direct from the *Campo Francesco Morosini* to the Accademia bridge to reach the

The famous spiral staircase in the courtyard of the Contarini del Bovolo palace. The alternating white stone and red brick brings to mind the Tower of Pisa.

Campo della Carità in front of the museum. However, if you have the time, don't hesitate to make the detour to Scala del Bovolo, described below.

From S. Stefano to the Scala del Bovolo

When you come out of the church of S. Stefano, follow the *Ferrovia-Piazzale Roma* arrows. Cross the **Campo S. Angelo,** from which you can catch a disturbing glimpse of the leaning campanile, and come out onto the **Campo Manin** where there is a Savings Bank, one of the few contemporary buildings in Venice (1968). A little street to the right will bring you to the Palazzo Contarini del Bovolo. Once inside the courtyard you can see the famous external spiral staircase. This is the **Scala del Bovolo** which was built in 1499 by Giovanni Candi who made skillful use of white stone and brick, but you may be surprised when you realize this famous structure, so often photographed and reproduced, stands in such a modest setting – a small courtyard which seems to house families of undernourished cats...

Now turn back to San Stefano and continue on your way to the Accademia.

▬ *THE ACCADEMIA*★★

Map III F-1-2 (Lines 1, 2 or 4: Accademia). *Open from 9 am – 2 pm, 1 pm on Sundays and holidays. Closed Mondays. Tel. 52-22-247.*

The *Gallerie dell'Accademia* is the finest art gallery in Venice and one of the most impressive museums in the world. It contains dozens of masterpieces by artists such as Carpaccio, Bellini, Giorgione, Titian, Tintoretto, Veronese, Palma, Bassano,. Piazzetta, Tiepolo, Guardi, Canaletto and Longhi. Painters who do not belong to the City of the Doges have not been overlooked – Cosimo Tura, Mantegna, Piero della Francesca, Memling – but the particular value of this museum is that it provides a complete panorama of the Venetian school. As you go from one room to the next, you see before you the evolution of the city's art, from the medieval Byzantine period to the landscapes of the 18th century by way of the Bellinian revolution (15th century) and the great Cinquecento (16th century).

For a survey of Venetian art and short biographies of the leading artists, refer to the section "Art in Venice" (*pp. 27-34*).

The buildings consist of the old church, the convent (don't hesitate to go into the courtyard for a look at the 1561 facade by Palladio) and the *Scuola of S. Maria delle Carità.*

Room I. At the top of the main staircase, beneath a 15th-century coffered ceiling, you will find works from the 13th, 14th and early 15th centuries. Byzantine influence, which dominates the mosaic work, and Gothic styles are combined in Paolo Veneziano's *Crowning of the Virgin with Scenes from the Lives of Jesus and St Francis* and in Lorenzo Veneziano's polyptychs of the *Annunciation* (1357 and 1371). *The Crowning of Mary in Heaven* (1438) by Jacobello del Fiore, was influenced (as were the works of M. Giambone and Niccolò di Pietro) by the Gothic style imported from Sienna.

Room II. This room was built at the end of last century for Titian's *Assumption* which is now at the *Frari*, but Room II contains several large altarpieces: **Virgin with Saints★★** (1485) in which Giovanni Bellini displays' his talent for strict composition while preserving the softness of light and forms; the *Vocation of the Sons of Zebediah*, by Marco Basaiti; *The Ten Thousand Martyrs of Mount Ararat*, by Carpaccio; *Virgin with an Orange between St Louis and St Jerome*, by Cima da Conegliano.

Room III. Works by Cima da Conegliano and Sebastiano del Piombo.

Rooms IV and V. These two small rooms are probably the most important in the museum, containing paintings of more modest proportions, but in such numbers that it takes your breath away. There are no fewer than 15 paintings on wood by Giovanni Bellini, all of the highest standard. The theme of the Virgin and Child is repeated many times over but each with a different approach, full of freshness and imagination; the soft light, delicacy of the drawing and colors are nothing short of sublime in such paintings as *Virgin and Child with St Catherine and St Magdalen*, *Virgin and Child with John the Baptist and a Saint* and *Madonna of the Trees*. The same quality appears in Bellini's *Redeemer*, his moving *Pietà* and the five little *Allegorical Figures* which have been identified as Luxury, Vanity, Inconstant Fortune, Infamy Unmasked and Fortune.

Other masterpieces include a *Virgin and Child* by Giovanni Bellini's father, Jacopo, *St Jerome*, an early work (*c.* 1450) by Piero della Francesca, the *Madonna of the Zodiac* by the Ferrarese Cosimo Tura (1445) and Hans Memling's *Portrait of a Youth in a Black Hat* from that other geographic pole of the Renaissance, Flanders.

Two other works deserve special mention: **St George,** a luminous painting on wood by Andrea Mantegna, Giovanni Bellini's brother-in-law and in some respects, his inspiration; and Giorgione's incomparable **Tempest**** — a strange painting by a mysterious artist. "By his use of color, he manages to create such an association between the figures and the background that the scenery enters into the action: a power emanates from the landscape which, however detailed, is conceived as a powerful whole. This may well be the true significance of this painting about which so much has been written. The title is descriptive and goes back to early days but what the subject really is has given rise to controversy. Some see it as a meeting between *King Adrastus* and *Queen Hypsypile*, inspired by a passage in *Statius' Thebaïs*; others simply see a pastoral idyll. Whichever it is, a storm is brewing and the threatening sky contrasts with the pensive look of the man and the domestic pose of the woman." (R. Pallucchini). A hidden aspect of the painting has recently been revealed by X-rays: a woman crouching by the brook once occupied the spot now taken by a man standing; Giorgione presumably decided that an upright figure would give better balance to his composition.

The subtle poetic mood of this painting is counterbalanced by the pitiless realism of *The Old Woman*.

Room VI. Here, we enter into the heyday of the 16th century with Titian's *St John the Baptist*, inspired by Michelangelo and introducing Mannerist elements. Another major painting from the time is Paris Bordone's *Fisherman Handing the Ring of St Mark to the Doge* (c. 1545).

Room VII. Lorenzo Lotto's **Portrait of a Young Man** (c. 1528) is one of his best works. He draws on all his sensitivity to depict this pensive lover of music, books and hunting. The still-life on the work table is truly sumptuous, his mastery of colors is evident and Lotto's whimsy is expressed in the little green lizard curled on a crumpled piece of fabric.

Room VIII. The *Sagra Conversazione*, an unfinished masterpiece by Palma the Elder (note the hands of St Catherine and St John the Baptist) is clearly reminiscent of Titian's classical style.

Room IX. Works of De Pitati and the Titian school.

Room X. The three most famous artists of the 16th-century Venetian school are represented here by several masterpieces: Titian, whose last work, the **Pietà** of 1576, expresses great despair through the domination of form and color by light (the canvas was restored in 1984); Tintoretto, whose *Translation of the Body of St Mark*, *The Miracle of St Mark* and *The Descent from the Cross*, were intended for the Scuola di S. Marco, show the master's taste for unusual theatrical compositions as well as his skill in obtaining dramatic effects through the opposition of light and shade; Veronese's enormous **Banquet in the House of Levi** (1573), a canvas measuring 42 ft × 18 ft/10.10 m × 5.55 m was intended to be a *Last Supper* until he was forced to change the title by the Inquisition which objected to the presence of Germans, jesters and dogs in this sacred scene. With Veronese, religious sentiment plays a secondary role; what really appealed to this amiable Venetian was color, a sumptuous setting and the richness of contemporary costumes.

Room XI. This room is largely devoted to Veronese. His **Mystical Marriage of St Catherine** is remarkable for the transparency of tones and the harmony of the whole; *Virgin and Saints* is a splendid canvas in which gold and silver contrast with more conventional colors to create a sense of joy. There are several Tintorettos as well: *Cain and Abel*, *Adam and Eve* and *The Creation of the Animals* (all three, c. 1553). In the first, violence is expressed by the clash of broken lines; the composition of the third is unusual: a series of receding horizontal planes which, in a way, foreshadows modern art.

The last giant of Venetian painting is Giambattista Tiepolo who displays his mastery of color and drawing, as well as a certain feeling for the fantastic, in the large **Punishment of Serpents** (c. 1720) and in the frescoes transferred from the church of the Scalzi.

Room XII. 18th-century landscape painters.

Room XIII. Paintings by Bassano, Palma the Younger and, above all, Tintoretto: outstanding portraits of *Doge Alvise Mocenigo* and *Procurator Jacopo Soranzo*.

Palaces and homes along the canals often show signs of decay but their colors reflected in the water, and the light playing along their facades, transform every scene into a painting.

Room XIV. The 17th century, although not to be compared with the previous century or the following, could still boast of several talented artists: Domenico Fetti (*David*), Bernardo Strozzi and Johann Liss.

Rooms XV, XVI and XVIa. Four of the Tiepolos displayed here were inspired by Ovid's *Metamorphoses*. The Alessandro Longhi painting, *Family of Procurator Luigi Pisani* (1758) does not lack in humorous touches. Piazzetta's *The Fortune-Teller* is an excellent genre painting which many people see as a portrait of Venice in all its final splendor.

Room XVII. Works by other great 18th-century artists are here. Canaletto's ambition was to depict his beloved city in its minutest detail; his precision is quite different from Francesco Guardi's nervous style and predilection for pale tints — dove gray, soft pink, blue-green and faded blue — with dashes of black (*Basin of S. Marco with S. Giorgio Maggiore and La Giudecca, Fire at The Oil Depot of S. Marcuola*). Note also the six little *Venetian Scenes* by Pietro Longhi, and Rosalba Carriera's delicate pastel portraits (*Portrait of a Boy*).

Room XVIII. (Corridor) 18th-century paintings: G. B. Tiepolo, P. Longhi, Fr. Zucarelli, *et al.* Also works by the young Canova and architectural studies.

Room XIX. After the 18th century, we return to the 15th century with works by Carpaccio and a copy of Antonello da Messina's *Annunciation*.

Room XX. Another high spot of the late 15th-century Venetian period is the cycle, **Miracles of the Relics of the Holy Cross★**, consisting of one panel by Carpaccio and 3 by Gentile Bellini. The latter's grandiose **Procession of the Relics in St Mark's Square★★** (1496) contains valuable information on daily life in Venice and on the architecture and the costumes of the day. The basilica is seen to be decorated with now-vanished mosaics, but the clock tower was not yet built. An equally fascinating slice of life is the *Miracle of the Relic Fallen into the S. Lorenzo Canal*, showing amphibious monks searching for the relic which has been accidentally dropped in the water.

Vittore Carpaccio's **Curing a Man Possessed** (1494) has the same pictorial qualities and documentary value. This is probably his best work and, in any case, certainly the most informative: we can see the Rialto bridge, built of timber, and so constructed as to open and let ships sail through (the present bridge was built a century later); there too are the gondolas, the chimneys with the same strange shapes they still have today and the roof terraces where women try, by sitting in the sun, to acquire the famous "Venetian blonde" hair color; but, above all, the crowd effects are superb.

Room XXI. This is reserved for the cycle of *The Legend of St Ursula*, painted between 1490 and 1496 by Carpaccio for the *Scuola di Sant'Orsola*. The most representative episodes are: *The Dream of St Ursula, The Arrival of St Ursula in Cologne*, and *The Arrival of the English Ambassadors*. Carpaccio constantly mixes reality and the imaginary, rearranges space – for instance, he dares put a caravel instead of a human figure in the foreground – and looks for new arrangements of geometric forms and colors.

Room XXIII. In the upper section of the former church of *S. Maria della Salute* there are four triptychs by Giovanni Bellini or from his workshop, three polyptychs by Bartolomeo Vivarini, a *Sagra Conversazione* by Alvise Vivarini and Carlo Crivelli's *St Jerome, St Augustine, St Peter and St Paul*.

Room XXIV. This is the former hall of the *Scuola* and has a carved and gilded Renaissance ceiling. There is a triptych by Antonio Vivarini and Giovanni d'Allemagna, and a very fine painting from Titian's classical period, *The Presentation of the Virgin* (1538). Thus, your visit ends with a view of the young Mary climbing the monumental stairs of the temple.

▬ FROM THE ACCADEMIA TO THE SALUTE

When you come out of the Accademia, turn left into Calle Contarini which will lead you to the *Rio S. Trovaso*. Follow it in a southerly direction and then cross it to reach the church of the same name.

Church of S. Trovaso

Map III F-1 (Lines 1, 2 or 4: Accademia, or 5: Zattere).

Rebuilt at the end of the 16th century in sober classical style, it contains a bas-relief attributed to Pietro Lombardo, and works by Tintoretto: in the chancel, *Joachim Driven from the Temple*; in the left-hand chapel, *The Temptation of St Anthony*; in the central chapel of the left transept, a *Last Supper* and *The Washing of Feet*. See also over the altar, a *Deposition* and *The Birth of the Virgin* by Palma the Younger.

On the bank of the Rio di S. Trovaso, you will pass the **Squero S. Trovaso,** a small gondola building and repair yard which goes back to the 17th century. It is one of only two in Venice. Gondolas are pulled up a ramp to be recaulked and repainted; the workshops contain various types of timber used in the construction of these renowned craft. The yard has been restored by the Italo-Bavarian Committee for the Protection of the Gondola.

The Zattere

The Rio di S. Trovaso links the Grand Canal and the *Zattere,* the wide sunfilled quays which provide a pleasant stopping place for walkers. While eating an ice cream, or even lunch, you can look at the quays of *La Giudecca*, 311 yds/300 m away, above which rises the majestic silhouette of Palladio's Redentore. For the Feast of the Redeemer (3rd weekend in July), a bridge of boats is put together to join the two banks. You may chance to see a large ship making its way along the wide *Giudecca* canal which is 29 ft/9 m deep.

The Church of the Gesuati

Also known as *S. Maria del Rosario* Map II D-2 (Line 5: Zattere). *Open to visitors daily from 8 am – 12 noon and from 5 – 7 pm.*

Built on the quayside, in front of an immense carpet of water, it has a certain grandeur. Designed by G. Massari and completed in 1736, it is known above all for its unusual *Tiepolo ceiling* in which the artist displays his gift for bold foreshortening: *Institution of the Rosary, Apotheosis of St Dominic, St Dominic Praying to the Virgin.* The ceiling was restored in 1975 by the French Committee. See also, by the first altar on the right, Tiepolo's *Virgin and Three Saints* (1740) and, by the third altar on the right, Piazzetta's masterpiece *The Dominicans* (1739); by the third altar on the left, Tintoretto's *Crucified Christ* (1570).

You will find, at the corner of the *Rio S. Vio* and the *Zattere,* the **Calcina** pensione where John Ruskin wrote part of his masterly work, *The Stones of Venice*. Turn left at this point to go along the *Rio* to *Campo S. Vio*. Take the *Calle Chiesa* on your right to reach the Palazzo Venier dei Leoni which now houses the Peggy Guggenheim collection.

Peggy Guggenheim Foundation★★

Map III F-2-3 (Lines 1: Salute, or 1, 2 or 4: Accademia). *Open April to October daily from 12 – 6 pm; free on Saturdays from 6 – 9 pm. Closed Tuesdays. Tel. 70-62-88.*

A remarkable personality who fell in love with Venice, Peggy Guggenheim set up this magnificent collection of modern art on the banks of the Grand Canal. After living in New York, England and France, this wealthy American heiress, wife of painter Max Ernst, bought the **Palazzo Venier dei Leoni,** a

The Grand Canal

strange edifice of which only the first floor had been completed. There is now an attractive terrace overlooking the Grand Canal and a superb garden where Peggy Guggenheim lies buried next to her beloved dogs.

The museum contains over 200 paintings and sculptures by more than 100 artists, representing every art movement of our times:

Cubism: Picasso, Braque, Marcel Duchamp, Fernand Léger, Jacques Villon, Juan Gris.

Futurism (especially the Italian School): Umberto Boccioni, Gino Severini, Giacomo Balla.

Abstract: Robert Delaunay, Kandinsky (*Landscape with Church*, 1913), Mondrian, Arp.

Dadaism and Surrealism: Max Ernst (*The Anti-Pope*, 1941), Giorgio de Chirico (*The Poet's Dream*, 1914), Chagall (*Rain*, 1911), Miró, Tanguy, Picabia, Man Ray, Dali (*Liquid Pleasures*, 1932), Magritte, Delvaux, Masson, Calder, Giacometti.

American Abstract: Pollock, Tobey.

There are also works by Francis Bacon and Henry Moore, and a series of 44 glass pieces from Murano establishing a link between the local craft and artists like Picasso, Le Corbusier, Ernst and Calder.

You will find it hard to resist sitting a while in the shady garden admiring how the sculptures merge with the vegetation: Takis' *The Signal*, Germaine Richier's *Tauromachie*, Brancusi's *Maïastra* and *Bird in Space*, and Eduardo Paolozzi's *Chinese Dog*.

The Point of the Salute

The *Calle del Bastion* passes in front of the **Church of S. Gregorio,** the Gothic apse and cloisters of which date from the 15th century. The church is now a restoration laboratory. Across the Rio della Salute rises the monumental church by Baldassare Longhena.

S. Maria della Salute★★ Map III F-3 (Line 1: Salute). *Open daily 8 am – 12 noon and 3 – 5 pm.* Erected as a public ex-voto following the terrible plague of 1630, this imposing Baroque octagonal edifice, which appears in innumerable views of Venice, including Canaletto's and Guardi's, owes part of its fame to its location on the bank of the Grand Canal: the steps of the portal come down almost to the edge of the water.

Erecting such a heavy monument presented enormous problems which were resolved in a quite astonishing manner, as G. Martinioni recounts in a fascinating and very precise work published in 1663: "They began by driving in 1,106,657 piles, 13 ft/4 m long, of oak, alder and larch. Across these piles they built a *zatterone* (a wooden floor like a raft) made of beams of oak and larch packed close together and securely tied. Then, with stones and mortar, they started to build the enormous edifice in accordance with the architect's plans."

Longhena's masterpiece, consecrated in 1687, has undergone extensive restoration work which was completed in 1976 and financed by the French Committee. This involved restoring and consolidating dozens of statues along the facade, replacing a number of essential parts of the structure, cleaning and refacing the outside and repairing the polychrome marble paving.

In the sacristy, you can admire the Tintoretto masterpiece, **The Wedding at Cana★**, an immense painting which produces an extraordinary sense of depth by a skillful use of perspective. The famous painting of the same name by Veronese, now in the Paris Louvre, was formerly in *S. Giorgio Maggiore.* There are three works by Titian, painted in 1543: *Cain and Abel, The Sacrifice of Abraham* and *David and Goliath*, as well as several of his less important paintings, among them the early *St Mark Enthroned, with Saints* (1512).

The **Dogana di Mare** (Maritime Customs House) stands at the point where the Grand Canal meets the *Giudecca* canal. This graceful 17th-century building, the work of Benoni, is surmounted by an enormous weathervane by Falcone (1659-1694), consisting of two bronze Telamones holding up a golden globe over which swivels a statue of Fortune.

ITINERARY D
NORTHERN VENICE BY WAY OF
THE RIALTO

This fourth itinerary will lead us to the northern part of
Venice, from St Mark's Square to the railway station or
the great parking area of *Piazzale Roma*, by way of the
Rialto, the Church of *Gesuiti*, *Ca' d'Oro*, the *Madonna
dell 'Orto*, the *Ghetto*, the *Cannaregio* canal and the
Scalzi church. It broadly corresponds to the signposted
itinerary from *S. Marco to Ferrovia*. We will indicate
those occasions when you should deviate temporarily
from that itinerary.

▬ *FROM ST MARK'S SQUARE TO THE RIALTO*

From St Mark's Square you can choose between the
Mercerie, lively but crowded thoroughfares that start under
the clock tower (*Merceria dell'Orologio*), or the *Calle dei
Fabbri* in the middle of the *Old Procuratie*. This street will take
you to the *Campo S. Luca*, a busy square and rendezvous
point for many Venetians (the *Standa* supermarket occupies
several buildings). From there you can enter the *Mercerie* on
your right to reach the *Campo S. Bartolomeo*, another
Venetian meeting point just in front of the Rialto. On your way,
you will come across the church of *S. Salvatore*.

The Church of S. Salvatore
Map III D-4 (Lines 1, 2 or 4: Rialto).

Built by Tullio Lombardo and completed by Sansovino between 1506 and 1534, it has a Baroque facade by G. Sardi
(1663) with statues by Falcone. Inside, there are two paintings
by Titian: the *Transfiguration* and the *Annunciation*. There is
also one by Giovanni Bellini, *The Supper at Emmaus*, notable
for its composition and the richness of the colors. During the
first half of August and on special religious feast days, visitors
are privileged to see a silver 14th-15th century altarpiece.

In **Campo S. Bartolomeo** Map III C-4 (Lines 1, 2 or 4: Rialto)
there is a clever *statue of Goldoni* by Antonio del Zotto. Carlo
Goldoni (1707-1793) is Venice's chief literary figure. Known as
the Italian Molière, he wrote more than a hundred plays.

To your left, the *Salizzada Pio X* brings you to the Rialto.

The Rialto Bridge

Map III C-4 (Lines 1, 2 or 4: Rialto)

Several wooden bridges had been constructed over the Canal, the earliest in 1180, before Antonio da Ponte built the present one between 1588 and 1592. It consists of a single arch, 158 ft long by 72 ft wide (48 m by 22 m). The overhanging portico, with its double row of shops, is a later addition. Building the bridge was no easy task, bearing in mind the nature of the soil and the need to design an arch high enough (24½ ft/7.50 m) to allow galleys to pass beneath.

The foundations rest on a clever arrangement of wooden piles. These *pali* are of two kinds: long ones (up to 11½ ft/3.50 m) resting on hard soil, and short ones (from 28 in to 6½ ft/70 cm to 2 m in length) very close to each other, which are intended to hold the earth – to "freeze" it. This heavy stone bridge thus rests on a complex wooden framework made up, on each bank, of 6000 piles driven below the level of the canal.

Extensive restoration work was carried out in 1977 by the Italian Committee *Venezia Nostra*. It included cleaning the vault of the arch and rebuilding part of the stonework and a section of the wooden framework, as well as renewing some of the lead roofing.

▬ *FROM THE RIALTO TO THE CA' D'ORO*

Coming back from Campo S. Bartolomeo, following the arrow signs *"Ferrovia"*, you reach the **Fondaco dei Tedeschi** (Map III C-4, Lines 1, 2 or 4: Rialto). This "Warehouse of the Germans" was rebuilt in 1580 by Scarpagnino. The facade is visible from the Rialto or indeed from a *vaporetto* (*see Itinerary A*). You can buy stamps here – it is now the central post office – and have a quick look at the delightful interior courtyard with its glass roof, a masterpiece of restraint.

Around S. Giovanni Crisostomo

Map III B-C-4 (Lines 1, 2 or 4: Rialto).

S. Giovanni Crisostomo is a church in the shape of a Greek cross, the last work of Mauro Codussi (1497-1504). It contains a masterpiece by Giovanni Bellini, **St Christopher, St Jerome and St Augustine** (1513) – see the first altar on the right – and a reredos by Sebastiano del Piombo, *St John Chrysostom with Other Saints* (1509). Behind the church stands the *Malibran Theater* (1678), dedicated in 1834 to the famous Spanish singer Maria Malibran. It is surrounded by arcaded houses and legend has it that Marco Polo was born either in one of them or in a house situated where the theater now stands.

The Church of SS. Apostoli (Map III B-4, Line 1: Ca' d'Oro), partly rebuilt in 1575 and altered in the 18th century, is worth a visit because of the fine painting by Tiepolo, *The Communion of St Lucia* (1748) on the altar of the Corner chapel.

The Gesuiti and the Fondamenta Nuove

Visitors in a hurry will go directly to the *Ca' d'Oro* by the *Strada Nuova*, others will make a short detour to the north to see the church of the Gesuiti. Follow the *Rio Terrà SS. Apostoli*, behind the church of the same name, then cross two bridges,

The remarkable Baroque facade of the church of the Gesuiti, also known as S. Maria Assunta, looks down on a quiet district.

to reach **S. Maria Assunta,** the **Church of the Gesuiti**★ (Map III A-5, Line 5: Fondamente Nuove; *open daily 10 am to midday and 5 – 7 pm*), built by Domenico Rossi between 1715 and 1730 from a design by G. B. Fattoretto thanks to a donation by the Manni family. It has one of the finest Baroque facades in Venice, adorned with statues of the twelve apostles. The interior decoration is quite extraordinary, from the fantastic patterns of green and white marble to the splendid olive-wood marquetry of the sacristy. This has been restored by the American Committee.

The remarkable painting by Titian, *The Martyrdom of St*

Market stalls are set up at the foot of the Rialto, where fish, vegetables and fruit from nearby islands give off enticing smells of the sea and countryside.

Lawrence (1508), is a major achievement in his career. The effect of light falling from heaven and the glow of the fire contrasting with the gloom of this nocturnal scene is quite extraordinary. This church also contains works by Tintoretto and Palma the Younger.

Beside the church, the **Fondamenta Nuove** is a wide quay with a splendid view over the lagoon and, in particular, the island of S. Michele, the great cemetery of Venice. Watch the sailing boats, rowing boats and motor launches go by and be grateful to the Italian authorities for having turned down the motorway which some people wanted to build along here by the Fondamenta Nuove.

Now turn back to the *Strada Nuova* and *the Ca' d'Oro.*

Ca' d'Oro, Galleria Giorgio Franchetti★

Map III B-3 (Line 1: Ca' d'Oro) *Open daily 9 am – 2 pm; 1 pm Sundays and holidays. Closed Mondays. Tel. 52-38-790.*

The facade of the **Ca' d'Oro,** which can be admired from the Grand Canal (*see Itinerary A, p. 75*), is the most beautiful Gothic palace in Venice. Although it has lost one wing, its layout recalls the style of Veneto-Byzantine residences, with a large hall and a central gallery corresponding to the water level portico where boats and gondolas used to moor. The *Contarini* family, who had it built during the first decade of the 15th century, entrusted to a group of master stonemasons the task of decorating its facade with richly mullioned galleries, windows with delicate tracery and stone lacework. The lavish gilt of this facade earned it the name of Golden House. After belonging to several Venetian and foreign families, this sumptuous residence was given to the State by the collector *Franchetti*. The interior decoration includes delicately carved ceilings and it is from inside the house that the visitor is able to appreciate fully the elegance of the Gothic windows, carved to produce a "lightness comparable to the finest lace." (R. Pallucchini).

The *Ca' d'Oro* was closed for years of extensive restoration: the walls had been affected by damp, the 16th-century golden ceiling and the works of art themselves were endangered. It has now been re-opened to the public who can visit the **Franchetti Gallery★** (a display of photographs in one of the first floor rooms outlines the progress of the restoration work). The result of this massive undertaking is nothing short of superb: the palace has recovered its former glory and its works of art are now displayed in accordance with the most up-to-date techniques, with careful lighting and standardized explanatory notices. Some may regret that it has now lost the charm of the *Ca' Rezzonico* or of the *Querini-Stampalia* art gallery which have retained their old disordered profusion and amateur look but modernization was the price of survival.

The collection, while not comparable to those of the Accademia or the Correr, includes some very fine pieces and several masterpieces by Renaissance artists. In the courtyard, note the splendid Verona red marble wellheads by Bartolomeo Bon (1427).

First Floor

The paintings include a *Virgin and Child* by Giovanni Bellini, an *Annunciation* and a *Death of the Virgin* by Vittore Carpaccio and others from his workshop, a *Passion* polyptych by A. Vivarini and the remarkable **St Sebastian★** by Andrea Mantegna, noteworthy for the sculptural treatment of the saint's body. There is an impressive display of bronzes (Andrea Briosco known as Riccio), medals by Pisanello (Francesco Sforza, John VIII Paleologus, Lionello d'Este) and tapestries. Finally, do not miss the **Double Portrait** of Tullio Lombardo who was perhaps the greatest Venetian sculptor of the early 16th century.

Second Floor

Going up one floor you advance in time; all the great Venetian masters are represented: Titian (*Venus*), Giorgione (frescoes from the Fondaco dei Tedeschi), Tintoretto (several portraits), Guardi. The north of Europe is also included, with numerous Flemish and Dutch works, Van Dyck's *Portrait of a Gentleman*, and *Portrait of a Man* by Corneille de Lyon, being particularly noteworthy.

▬▬ *FROM THE CA' D'ORO TO THE STATION*

On the bank of the *Rio di Noale*, the **Giovanelli Palace** (Map III A-3, Line 1: Ca' d'Oro), boasts an extraordinary 15th-century Gothic facade with stone lacework reminiscent of the Palace of the Doges. A little further along the *Strada Nuova*, the *Correr*, another 15th-century palace, faces the **Church of S. Fosca** which, although rebuilt in the 17th century, retains its 15th-century campanile. Turn right after passing the church to reach the *Madonna dell'Orto*.

Madonna dell'Orto★ Map II A-3 (Line 5: Madonna dell' Orto). *Open 9 am – 12 noon and 3 – 5 pm*. The beautiful facade of this 15th-century Gothic church is decorated with statues by the Dalle Masegne and Bon schools. Note the elegant portal showing the transition between the Gothic and Renaissance styles, with a statue of St Christopher by B. Bon.

It owes its name, "Our Lady of the Garden", to a miraculous statue of the Virgin found in a nearby garden. Tintoretto, Cima da Conegliano and Giovanni Bellini all contributed to the decoration, and Tintoretto is buried here (first chapel on the right). On the first altar is Cima's **St John the Baptist and Other Saints** (1493); Bellini's **Virgin and Child** (1478) is in the first chapel. This masterpiece was restored by the American Committee, damaged by thieves and once more repaired in 1972. However, this is really Tintoretto's church: his **Presentation of the Virgin** hangs above the entrance to the S. Mauro chapel, *Saint Agnes Resuscitating Licinius* on the altar of the Contarini chapel, his *Last Judgement* and *Adoration of the Golden Calf* are in the chancel, his *Martyrdom of St Christopher*, *Virtues* and *Apparition of the Holy Cross* are in the apse.

The Ghetto

Instead of retracing your steps, we suggest that you cross the *Rio Madonna dell'Orto* and the *Rio della Sensa* (on the banks of which stands Tintoretto's house where he died in 1594) and walk along the *Fondamenta degli Ormesini* in a westerly direction, thus reaching the **Campo Ghetto Nuovo** (Map II A-B-2), a wide square surrounded by the "skyscrapers" of Venice (rising to a mere five or six stories!).

Originally, the Jewish district was the island of La Giudecca, but the Most Serene Republic moved several thousand of its residents when the church of *Il Redentore* was being built. The Jews were resettled in the **Ghetto Vecchio** which spread to include the Ghetto Nuovo. Lack of space compelled the inhabitants to build taller houses. The word ghetto is said by some to come from the Venetian *geto*, a foundry; in time it was applied to any Jewish district in Europe.

There are five synagogues all at least one floor above street level. The Venetian government allowed Jews to practise their religion but forbade all proselytizing. The synagogue on the *Campo Ghetto Vecchio* was built in 1655 by Longhena.

The **Museo Ebraico** is situated on the *Campo Ghetto Nuovo*. *Open 10 am – 12.30 pm. Closed Saturdays, Sunday after-noons and on Jewish holidays. Tel. 71-50-12).*

The Cannaregio Canal

From the *Ghetto Vecchio*, you come out on the banks of the *Cannaregio Canal*. You will find few tourists in this district, but several remarkable buildings.

The **Palazzo Surian Bellotto,** (Map II A-1, Line 5: Ponte Tre Archi). This palazzo, built by Sardi (16th century), is situated at the end of the canal before the lagoon. The famous French philosopher Jean-Jacques Rousseau stayed here when he was secretary to the French Ambassador whose residence this was. The **Ponte Tre Archi** (three-arched bridge), which was the work of Andrea Tirali (1688), seems too large for this quiet district but it provided dry-footed access to the Ambas-sador's residence.

The **Church of S. Giobbe**★ Map II B-2 (Line 5: Ponte Tre Archi). *Open 8.30 am – 12 noon, 3.30 – 6 pm.* The church was begun at the end of the 15th century and completed by Pietro Lombardo who added a few Renaissance touches to its portal. It consists of a single nave with chapels along one side: the first is in the Lombard style, the second is Tuscan with a vaulted roof decorated with Della Robbia terracottas. Over the last altar, on the right, Paris Bordone's *St Andrew, St Peter and St Nicolas*. Close by is the ogival *Chapel Contarini* and the coffered-ceiling sacristy; at the back, you can see *The Annunciation*, a triptych by A. Vivarini and G. Alemagna. The sanctuary is a fine creation in the Renaissance style by P. Lombardo; the stalls date from the 16th century. Note in particular the *tombstone of Doge Cristoforo Moro*, a master-piece of Lombard sculpture and, on the right of the church, a cloister gallery.

The **Palazzo Labia**★ Map III A-1 (Line 5: Ponte Guglie). Palazzo Labia is one of the finest private 18th-century buildings in Venice. The imposing facade overlooking the *Rio* is in Istrian stone (Andrea Cominelli, 1720) and is decorated with three types of columns but the other facade, by Tremignon, is more simple (1750). Although the palace's architecture is admirable, it owes its fame largely to the Tiepolo *frescoes* in the main first-floor drawing room but, unfortunately, it is not open to the public.

From the *Campo S. Geremia*, the *Lista di Spagna* leads to the Church of the Scalzi near the railway station and opposite the *Scalzi bridge*.

Gli Scalzi★

Map II B-2 (Lines 1, 2, 4 or 5: Ferrovia). *Open 6.30 am – 12 noon and 3.30 – 7 pm.*

Situated in front of the three bridges that cross the Grand Canal, this "Church of the Barefoot Carmelites" – or, to give it its official name, *S. Maria di Nazareth* – was built according to a design by Longhena (c. 1675) with a facade by G. Sardi. It is a very successful essay in the Baroque style with two sets of twin columns and statues attributed to B. Falcone. The rich interior includes polychrome marble and gilt; the main altar is set under a baldachin. The immense painting on the ceiling (1934) replaces a Tiepolo fresco destroyed in 1915. In the second chapel on the right, a fine altar is dominated by Tiepolo's fresco *The Glorification of St Theresa*; on the walls, there are paintings by N. Bambini. In the first chapel on the left, you can see frescoes by Tiepolo.

ITINERARY E
THE CHARM OF THE QUIET DISTRICTS

The districts of S. Polo, S. Croce and Dorsoduro, east of the Grand Canal, are quieter than S. Marco on the opposite side. There are fewer tourists and gift shops, and more residents and traditional businesses but there are just as many historic and artistic sites. This itinerary includes at least two important churches, S. Maria Gloriosa dei Frari and S. Sebastiano, a superb *scuola*, S. Rocco, and several museums, including the handsome Ca' Rezzonico.

This itinerary could be considered as an extension of Itineraries C and D. What's more, you can change from Itinerary C to E at any time simply by crossing the Grand Canal by the *traghetti* gondolas that link the two banks between any of the following places:

Palazzo Garzoni / Palazzo Dolfin
S. Benedetto / The Madonnetta
The Fondamenta del Carbon / The Riva del Vin
S. Sofia / The Pescheria
The Calle della Regina / S. Felice
S. Stae / The Maddalena
S. Marcuola / The Palazzo Correr
S. Geremia / The Riva di Biasio

▬ FROM THE RIALTO TO THE FRARI

The walk begins in a very lively district, near the Rialto Bridge (*see Itinerary D, p. 112*). From the bridge, and more especially from the *Riva del Vin*, you can see the line of *palazzi* along the canal on the opposite side: from the bridge, the *Manin* (Bank of Italy), *Bembo* (15th-century Gothic in red brick), *Dandolo*, *Loredan* (town council; a Veneto-Byzantine palace built over a gallery), *Corner Martinengo* (Tourist Office; 18th century; orange roughcast plaster).

The commercial area extends from the *Pescheria* (fish market) along the *Ruga degli Orefici* and dates from the first days of Venice's trade. The *Fabbriche Vecchie* (16th century) along the street used to be the offices of the merchants and shipowners. "In the earliest times the *Rialto* (the high shore) had been chosen because of its high level and because, as a commercial center and the seat of the *Banco Giro* (from the 12th century), it afforded better protection. The fruit and vegetable market filled the *ruga* while the arcades sheltered jewelers' shops renowned for their delicate and graceful work." (R. Pallucchini).

The Church of S. Giacomo di Rialto Map III C-4 (Lines 1, 2 or 4: Rialto), on the right of the *ruga*, is believed to be one of the oldest in Venice (4th-5th century), but it really dates from the 11th-12th century and was almost entirely rebuilt in the 17th. It was designed in the shape of a Greek cross, with cupolas; the capitals date from the 10th century. On the right altar, you can see M. Vecellio's *Annunciation* and over the main altar, Vittoria's *St James the Apostle* is in marble.

Against one of the arcades of the *Campo di Rialto*, in front of the church, stands the *Pietra del Bando*, a short pillar of pink granite from which laws and notices affecting the life of the city were proclaimed. The little staircase next to it is held up by a 16th-century telamon.

About 110 yards/100 m from the *Pescheria* stands the **Church of S. Cassiano** (Map III B-3), notable for its 12th-century campanile and its works by Tintoretto (*Resurrection, Descent into Limbo*). From there you go to the Pesaro Palace with its museum of modern art and the Oriental museum.

Palazzo Pesaro★

Map III B-2-3 (Line 1: S. Stae).

This 17th-century palace is a sumptuous edifice designed by Longhena. The concave facade curves elegantly along the Grand Canal. Although a Baroque building, it is distinctly restrained, in the style of Sansovino (*see Itinerary A, p. 75*).

Galleria d'Arte Moderna
Currently undergoing repairs; inquire at the Tourist Office or call 52-24-543 to check on opening hours. This gallery, founded in 1897, continues to grow, thanks to gifts and regular purchases at the Bienniale exhibitions. Part of the collection consists of works from the last century, but the majority are contemporary paintings and sculptures. Most of the artists are Italian but you will find here, to name only the best known, paintings by Troyon, Bonnard, Corot, Rafaelli, Kisling, Rouault, Vlaminck, Chagall, Dufy, Manessier, Marquet, Zadkine, Klee, Ernst, Miró and Kandinsky. Italian artists include Giorgio de Chirico, Carlo Carrà, Zandomeneghi, Grigoletti and, above all, Medardo Rosso, who is represented by 10 remarkable paintings. Among the sculptors we should mention are Rodin, Bourdelle, Calder and Henry Moore.

Museo Orientale★ *Also undergoing repairs; for opening hours inquire at the Tourist Office or call tel. 52-27-681*. This gallery contains the largest Italian collection of Far Eastern paintings, sculptures, weapons and costumes, with particular emphasis on items from Japan.

The Church of S. Stae Map III A-B-2 (Line 1: S. Stae). A few steps from the Pesaro Palace, at the edge of the Grand Canal, this church has a luxuriant 1709 Baroque facade. Inside, paintings include an early work by Tiepolo, *The Martyrdom of*

St Bartholomew, and a *Martyrdom of St James the Elder* by Piazzetta. Three statues by Corradini stand in the entablature of the portal — *Faith*, the *Redeemer* and *Hope*. Entirely restored, from its foundation to its roof, it is today frequently used for concerts.

S. Giacomo dell 'Orio Map III B-2 (Line 1: S. Stae or Rivia di Basio). *Open 8 am – 12 noon and 5 – 7 pm.*

To reach the *Frari*, you will pass through the delightful *Campo S. Giacomo dell 'Orio*. The little church of that name, founded in the 9th century and partly rebuilt in the 16th century, has retained its structure and some medieval features (apse). The nave has a timber ceiling shaped like an upturned keel (16th century). The side aisles are separated by irregular pillars and this, together with the mixture of styles and periods in the sanctuary, produce an attractive interior. The 16th-century organ is adorned with paintings by A. Schiavone. Over the main altar, you will find Lorenzo Lotto's *Madonna with Saints* (1546); under the triumphal arch, a great *Christ* (14th century) painted on wood by Paolo Veneziano; in the *sagrestia vecchia* (old sacristy), there are paintings by Palma the Younger. In the *sagrestia nuova* (new sacristy), the ceiling is by Veronese, while the paintings on the walls are by Giovanni Buonconsiglio, Francesco Bassano and A. Schiavone.

You can then go on to the church of the *Frari* which emerges, rising to its full height, out of the shady narrow streets and the silent canals.

▬ AROUND THE FRARI

The church of S. Maria dei Frari, with the Scuola di S. Rocco on its southern side, is one of Venice's great artistic attractions. Even if you are short of time, don't be satisfied with seeing only St Mark's and the Rialto. Visit this superb district: you will not regret it.

S. Maria Gloriosa dei Frari★★

Map III C-D-1 (Line 1: S. Tomà). Unlike the other churches in Venice, *an admission fee is charged. Open from Easter to September 30 from 9 am – 12 noon, 2.30 – 6.30 pm, Sundays 3 – 6.30 pm. Off-season: 9.30 am – 12 noon, 3 – 5.30 pm, Sundays 3 – 5.30 pm.*

This is the largest church in Venice, built between 1338 and 1443, and dominated by a campanile in the Venetian style of 1396. Titian and Monteverdi are buried here, and the heart of Canova is here, too, in a porphyry vase. "The *Frari* were the Minor Friars of the Franciscan order who came to Venice in 1222 and erected their first church in the first half of the 14th century oriented in the opposite direction to the present one.

"A new church was begun in the middle of the 14th century, starting with the apse; the Gothic facade was completed during the Renaissance. The imposing interior consists of a triple nave with a central chancel for the friars. This was closed off by a marble barrier decorated with Gothic motifs, bas-reliefs and statues which reflect the spirit of the Renaissance." (R. Pallucchini).

S. Maria Gloriosa dei Frari, the largest church in Venice, is a kind of pantheon of the city's great figures. The monumental well in the cloisters is the work of Palladio (1713).

Along the right-hand aisle, you can see, in turn, the altar of St Anthony, by Longhena, with statues by J. Le Court; the mausoleum of Titian (19th century); on the second altar, Salviati's *Presentation of the Virgin* (1548) and the monument of A. Este (1666); the altar of St Joseph with a *St Jerome*, a statue by Vittoria, and a funeral monument of the 16th century; the altar of St Catherine with a painting by Palma the Younger, then three funeral monuments; above the cloister door is a wooden sarcophagus which, according to tradition, is by the Condottiere Carmagnola; opposite, you can see a 17th-century chest and, above, paintings by A. Vicentino.

In the straight transept, right, the Jacopo Marcello monument by P. Lombardo (15th century), sober in design but richly ornamented; also note the monument to Fra Pacifico, the companion of St Francis (1437); above the sacristy door, a monument to B. Pesaro; on the left, a monument to P. Savelli attributed to J. della Quercia. You will discover in the sacristy one of Giovanni Bellini's finest Madonnas "gentle and royal, like a Byzantine Eleussa", in the center of the **triptych of the Virgin with Saints,** with, on the left *St Nicholas and St Peter* and, on the right, *St Benedict and St Francis*. This sacristy, as large as a church, contains an unusual 17th-century clock carved from a single block of cypress wood.

From there, you enter the chapter room: monument to the Doge F. Dandolo with Veneziano's *Presentation of the Doge and His Wife to the Virgin by St Francis*. Through the sacristy windows you can glimpse the cloister designed by Palladio, with a monumental well (1713).

On the way back, notice in the chapels on the right: *Virgin with Child and Saints* by B. Vivarini (1482), two Gothic funeral monuments and the superb polychrome statue of **St John the Baptist.** The signature of Donatello and the date, 1483, long concealed by a coat of brown paint, were revealed in the course of restoration.

Chancel: between two tall bay windows which stress the verticality of the architecture, you will find the **Assumption** (1518), Titian's splendid masterpiece which Canova once called the finest painting in all the world. The boldness of the composition on three planes, depicting the Virgin on clouds crowded with angels, is equalled only by the skillful interplay of the two dominant colors of the picture: red and gold. Restoring it proved such a difficult task that it became necessary to set up a laboratory inside the church to clean away the varnish and destructive parasites.

On the side wall, to the left, you can see the Renaissance mausoleum of Doge N. Tron (1476) by A. Rizzo; facing it, the monument to Doge F. Foscari by N. di Giovanni.

In the left apsidal chapel, you will find paintings by Palma the Younger and A. Vincentino, the monument to A. Travisan (1500), the altarpiece by A. Vivarini completed by M. Basaiti, *St Ambrosio with Angel Musicians and Saints*, and the tomb of Claudio Monteverdi, choirmaster of S. Marco, who died in 1643.

Left transept: Gothic wooden altarpiece (15th century), funeral monument to G. Orsini in the Lombard style; in the

Corner chapel, mausoleum of F. Corner, a Renaissance work attributed to the Donatello school; over the baptismal font, a marble *St John the Baptist*, by Sansovino (1554); above the altar, *St Mark with Angel Musicians and Saints*, a triptych by B. Vivarini (1474).

Left aisle: a 17th-century coffer and paintings by A. Vincentino: opposite, the strange *Franciscan Tree* which groups together the saints and famous figures of the order; after the *Emiliani* chapel, on the second altar you come to the **Ca' Pesaro Madonna,** a magnificent work by Titian (1526) notable for the boldness of color and the Virgin's extraordinarily luminous white veil. Framing the side door, the mausoleum of Doge P. Pesaro, from a design by Longhena, and the 1827 monument to A. Canova, a work carried out by students from a sketch made by the master for a monument to Titian.

In the center of the church, the outside of the chancel is Gothic with marble bas-reliefs by the Bons and Lombaros which herald the coming of the Renaissance. The 124 stalls are the work of Mauro Cozzi (1468).

The Scuola Grande di S. Rocco★★

Map III D-1 (Line 1: S. Tomà). *Open daily 9 am – 1 pm and 3.30 – 6.30 pm during the season; from 10 am – 1 pm off-season. Tel. 34-864.*

This superb building dedicated to S. Rocco is one of the largest and richest *scuole* of Venice. Built in Renaissance style by Bon and Scarpagnino during the first half of the 16th century, it has a beautiful facade with Corinthian pillars and a frieze with allegorical figures. It owes its fame to the fact that it retains its original decorations, an incomparable set of paintings by Tintoretto specially painted for the Confraternity. It could be said that this is to Tintoretto what the Sistine Chapel is to Michelangelo.

"With a seemingly inexhaustible imagination, Tintoretto interpreted incidents from the *Old* and the *New Testaments* in accordance with a pattern of symbolism adapted to the religious and charitable aims of the Confraternity. He created a world of his own, intense, transfigured and renewing the traditions of pictorial expression, carrying to its highest point the struggle between color and form in the revelation of light." (R. Pallucchini).

The interior, with 56 Tintoretto paintings, marble decorations and carved paneling, is an artistic treasure house. The ground floor, reserved for scenes from the *New Testament*, has a statue of *S. Rocco* by G. Campagna over the altar and paintings of *The Annunciation*, the *Adoration of the Magi, The Flight into Egypt, The Massacre of the Innocents, St Mary Magdalen, St Mary of Egypt, The Circumcision, The Assumption.*

The upper room is an amazing place, firstly because of its size, but chiefly because all the walls and ceilings are hung with paintings by Tintoretto – ask for a mirror so that you can view at your leisure without risking a crick in the neck.

On the ceiling, episodes from the *Old Testament: Adam and Eve, Moses's Rod, Moses's Vision, Column of Fire, Jonah and* the Whale, The Miracle of the Bronze Serpent, Ezekiel's Vision, Jacob's Ladder, The Sacrifice of Isaac, Manna Falling from Heaven, Elisha and the Loaves, Elijah Fed by the Angel, The Passover (1576-1578).

Along the walls, scenes from the New Testament: S. Rocco, S. Sebastiano, The Nativity, Baptism, Resurrection, Prayer in the Garden of Olives, The Last Supper, The Miracle of the Loaves, Resurrection of Lazarus, Ascension, The Pool of Siloam, The Temptation of Christ (1578-1581).

See also Tintoretto's self-portrait.

The great masterpiece of the scuola is in the Sala dell'Albergo at the back of the main room on the left: the immense **Crucifixion**★★★ is a work of great power and intensity restored through an American grant. In the same room, examine the Apotheosis of S. Rocco on the ceiling, The Way of the Cross, Ecce Homo and, above all, the startling **Christ Before Pontius Pilate.** Displayed on easels, you will also see Tintoretto's Christ Bearing the Cross and Titian's Dead Christ.

Don't leave the area without visiting the **church of S. Rocco** next door. The facade is inspired by that of the Scuola and it contains further remarkable Tintoretto paintings.

Finally, in a lighter vein, go and see the unusual windmills which the locals have erected on their balconies just behind the Scuola (take the Calle Tintoretto).

▬ FROM THE FRARI TO THE CA' REZZONICO

Map II C-2, (Line 1: S. Tomá). South of the Frari, the **Church of S. Pantalon** has a luminous trompe-l'œil ceiling (the biggest in Venice) by Antonio Fumiani and you can see The Triumph of the Eucharist, a remarkable unsigned work of the 18th century, as well as The Coronation of Mary (1444) by Antonio Vivarini and Giovanni d'Alemagna.

At the vast Campo S. Margherita you have two options: go directly to Ca' Rezzonico by the Rio Terrà Canal, or make a detour towards the south-west which is well worthwhile because, at the end of the campo, you will find the Church and Scuola dei Carmini.

I Carmini

Map II D-1 (Lines 1: Rezzonico, or 5: S. Basilio).

The Gothic **church of S. Maria del Carmine** (open 9 am – 12 noon and 4 – 7.30 pm) possesses a Renaissance facade of rare sobriety. Go inside for the Adoration of the Shepherds (1509), a masterpiece by Cima da Conegliano. Also on view are Lorenzo Lotto's St Nicholas (1529) and Padovinano's St Liberale (1638). Restoration has been undertaken by the International Fund for Monuments, Venice Committee U.S.A.

The **Scuola Grande dei Carmini** (open 9 am – 12 noon, 3 – 6 pm. Closed Sundays and holidays) is situated opposite the church. Built in the 17th century along the lines of the other scuole, it has two facades by Longhena. The decoration dates from the 18th century and consists, in the main, of eight Tiepolo canvases along the ceiling of the upper room, the most impressive being The Virgin Offering the Scapular to the

Blessed Simeone Stock. Admire, too, the *Judith and Holophernes* by Piazzetta. The American Committee has been active in carrying out restoration work, strengthening the ceilings, cleaning the facades, repairing paintings and wrought iron and waterproofing the ground floor of the chapel.

There are three other interesting churches a short distance from the *Scuola dei Carmini*, and, in addition, this relatively empty, almost desolate quarter of Venice provides the visitor with a different impression of the city, off the beaten track.

One of the oldest churches in Venice (7th century), at the end of the *Rio S. Nicolò*, the **church of S. Nicolò dei Mendicoli** (Map II D-1, Line 5: S. Basilio) is surrounded by abandoned warehouses and tumbledown houses. Although remodeled on several occasions, it still has its 12th-century campanile. Its rich Baroque decorations warrant a visit, as does *St Nicholas Giving his Blessing* a superb wooden figure (15th century) in the chancel.

Retracing your steps, you reach **S. Angelo Raffaele** (Map II D-1, Line 5: S. Basilio). Built in the 7th century and remodeled in the 17th century, it is attractively situated by the *rio* of the same name and has a graceful facade of 1735 with, above the portal, a 16th-century group, *Tobias and Raphael*. Inside, below the organ, paintings by Francesco or Antonio Guardi (both of these attributions have their supporters) depicting the story of Tobias, one of the most remarkable series of paintings of the 18th-century Venetian School.

The most impressive of the three churches is *S. Sebastiano*, behind *S. Angelo Raffaele*, largely because of the quality of its decoration.

S. Sebastiano★★

Map II D-1 (Line 5: S. Basilio). *Open 10 am – 12 noon and 4 – 6 pm on Sundays and holidays.*

Rebuilt in the 16th century by Scarpagnino, the building is filled with paintings by Veronese, which makes this church as important for lovers of his work as the Scuola Grande di S. Rocco is for admirers of Tintoretto – more so in fact, because the paintings on display here represent almost the entire career of Veronese. Lighting is available on payment of a small charge, and mirrors may be hired to view the ceiling frescoes without discomfort.

It is the ceiling which will first attract your attention with the three masterpieces: *Esther Before Ahasuerus, The Crowning of Esther* and *The Triumph of Mordecai*. Other works on display are: *Virgin, St Catherine and a Monk* (first altar on the right), *Virgin with St Sebastian and Other Saints* (chancel, center), *Martyrdom of St Sebastian* (chancel, right) and *Martyrdom of St Mark and St Marcellinus* (chancel, left). Other artists represented in S. Sebastiano are Paris Bordone and Titian. Lastly, do not forget to visit the sacristy for its ceiling decorated with the *Evangelists*.

This church is, appropriately enough, the burial place of Veronese; his tomb is in the left side-aisle.

To reach the *Ca' Rezzonico*, take the *Calle Avogaria*, then the *Calle Lunga S. Barnaba*.

Ca' Rezzonico: Museo del Settecento Veneziano★

Map III E-1 (Line 1: Rezzonico). *Open 10 am – 4 pm; 9 am – 12.30 pm Sundays and holidays. Closed Fridays. Tel. 52-24-543.*

This handsome palace could be a twin of the Ca' Pesaro (*see Itinerary A, p. 75*), because it, too, is the work of the great Baroque architect, Baldassare Longhena, although the upper story is by G. Massari (18th century). Its art collection is one of the best and most appealing and concentrates on that century.

Go up by the great Massari staircase to the reception hall adorned with Crosato frescoes (18th century) and furniture by Brustolon. In the next rooms, you can see: furniture of Venetian lacquer with Chinese motifs, 18th-century knick-knacks, paintings and chandeliers; two Tiepolo ceilings (**Merit Between Virtue and Nobility** and **Wisdom and Strength**), two others with medallions by Maffei and Guarana; pastels by Rosalba Carriera.

On the second floor, look at paintings by Piazzetta, Lys, Zais, Zuccarelli and Pellegrini but do not miss the small paintings that make up the **Scenes of Venetian Life** by P. Longhi, especially the *Moorish Ambassador* whose startling red costume stands out so effectively against the softer tones of the rest of that painting. Note also the two masterpieces by Guardi, the *Sisters' Visiting Room* and, especially, **Il Ridotto,** remarkable for the bearing and the animation of the masked figures. See also the restored *New World* frescoes, by Gian Domenico Tiepolo.

The third floor, which, unfortunately, has been closed to visitors for some years, contains the reconstruction of an 18th-century pharmacy, a small puppet theater, costumes, knick-knacks and a collection of porcelain and faience.

ITINERARY F
WHERE VENICE IS A VILLAGE

The districts to the east of *S. Marco*, between the *Fondamenta Nuove* in the north and the *Riva degli Schiavoni* in the south, are worth a detailed visit because of their particular charm and also for their artistic treasures. They include several superb churches, such as *S. Zaccaria* and *SS. Giovanni e Paolo*, the marvelous *Scuola di S. Giorgio degli Schiavoni*, and two important museums, the *Museo Storico Navale* and the *Querini-Stampalia* Gallery. The further you get from *S. Marco*, the more the crowds thin out and the streets acquire a village atmosphere. Continue on to the south-east and you can enjoy the peace of the *Giardini Pubblici* (Public Gardens), a setting of quiet greenery which seems oddly out of place in this city of stone and water.

▬ *FROM ST MARK'S SQUARE TO SS. GIOVANNI E PAOLO*

The **Riva degli Schiavoni** Map III E-6 (Lines 1, 2, 4, 5 or 8: S. Zaccaria) which follows on from the *Molo*, facing the midday sun, is where you are most aware of Venice's maritime past. You are at once struck by the intense activity on the *S. Marco* basin, whether it be the tireless motorboats, the proud tugs which bring to mind stately ships about to leave for distant shores, or the liveliness of the café terraces and the ceaseless flow of pedestrians which add the flavor of a Mediterranean port to the scene.

Walk along in front of the Bridge of Sighs (*see Itinerary B, p. 83*), cross the *Rio del Vin* and take the little *calle* with the sign "*S. Zaccaria*". Then follow the signposted walk (*Ospedale*, hospital) to the *Scuola di S. Marco* next to the church of *SS. Giovanni e Paolo*.

S. Zaccaria★

Map III D-E-6 (Lines 1, 2, 4, 5 or 8: S. Zaccaria). *Open 10 am – 12 noon, 4 – 6 pm.*

Situated in a quiet tree-shaded square, this church was founded in the 9th century and rebuilt in the 15th century by Gambello and Codussi. The Renaissance facade is one of the finest in all Venice. The Veneto-Byzantine *campanile* is 13th century. The houses on the northern side of the square were transformed from a gallery of the old cloister of the abbey, the gardens of which used to stretch as far as St Mark's Square.

The appeal of the interior is due, in particular, to Giovanni Bellini's excellent **Virgin and Child with Saints** (1505, restored in 1975) over the left chapel. To be quite sure of appreciating its rich colors, take a few coins with you: it would be a pity if you were unable to operate the lighting system. The valuable *Callido organ* has been restored by the Netherlands Committee. Other chapels have works deserving your attention: the *Chapel of St Athanasius* (right) has paintings by Palma the Elder (*Virgin with Saints*) and Tintoretto (*The Birth of St John*) as well as a *Crucifixion* attributed to Van Dyck; on the altar you can see Titian's *Addolorata*; on the vault of the *Chapel of S. Tarasio*, the chancel of the earlier church, there are *frescoes* by A. del Castagno (*Eternal Father and Saints*, 1442, restored in 1970). These are rare in that they reveal a Tuscan influence in a Venetian *milieu*. Do not miss the three sumptuous polyptychs by A. Vivarini and G. d'Alemagna.

Some 328 yards/300 m north of S. Zaccaria the vast **Campo S. Maria Formosa** displays its *palazzi* — *Malipiero-Trevisan*, *Priuli* (1580) and the double Gothic-style *Donà* — and is the site of a very lively market.

The church of **S. Maria Formosa** Map III C-D-5 (Lines 1, 2, 4, 5 or 8: S. Zaccaria or 1, 2, or 4: Rialto), built in 1492 by *Mauro Codussi* and rebuilt in the 17th century, has two remarkable 16th-century facades. Inside, admire Palma the Elder's early work, *St Barbara with Saints* (1509), notable for the sense of majesty that emanates from the fair-headed saint. The parish has recently made an urgent appeal to UNESCO and private committees to assist with renovating the roof of the church and plaster-work.

Slightly back from *Campo S. Maria Formosa*, to the south of the church, you will find the small *Campiello Querini*, along which runs a *rio* dominated by the famous *Palazzo Querini-Stampalia*.

Querini-Stampalia Palace

Map III D-5 (Lines 1, 2, 4, 5 of 8: S. Zaccaria or 1, 2, or 4: Rialto). *Open 10 am – 3.45 pm; Sundays and holidays from 10 am – 2.45 pm. Closed Mondays. Tel. 52-25-235.*

The *palazzo* was built in the 16th century, the interior was remodeled in the 19th century. The architect, Scarpa, gave it new life by restoring its interior space which was compartmentalized during the 19th century. Various passageways provide access and a sense of openness. The palace is now greatly animated and it is possible to visualize what life was like in those great houses which were entered by boat. Better still, a modern decor making use of period decorative elements has ensured the success of this restoration, linking contemporary forms and materials with traditional ones. Brought to life by the action of light and water, the palace also retains its vitality because it is open to young people and students. It is the central office of the important *Fondazione*

From time to time, it is pleasant to leave the bustle of the canals and walk along the narrow streets, to mingle with Venetians.

Scientifica Querini-Stampalia founded in 1869 around a valuable library and the family art collection.

The Library consists of 230,000 books and a great collection of 18th-century newspapers and periodicals, It is a working library, something which is not common in Italy where libraries are usually book museums. In recent years it has increased its collection with books on a wide variety of subjects.

An American committee has supervised the maintenance of the library premises; it is now working on maintaining the galleries.

On the second floor, the **Pinacoteca**★ offers a complete panorama of Venetian painting from the 14th-18th centuries. It is particularly rich in the works of Pietro Longhi and has a good portrait collection. A visit will enable you to appreciate the evolution of painting in Venice.

The first room contains a series of anecdotal works depicting daily life in Venice. Many of these scenes have touches of humor, especially the painting which shows the *Rialto* at "rush hour".

Paintings of special note include a *Crowning of the Virgin* by C. and D. Veneziano, a **Presentation at the Temple** by Giovanni Bellini and a *Virgin and Child* by Lorenzo di Credi. Then see the *Sagra Conversazione* by Palma the Elder and Judith by Vincenzo Catena. Among the paintings by Pietro Longhi, stop a moment to view the series of the Seven Sacraments, especially the *Baptism*, the **Geography Lesson** and the surprising **Hunt in a Valley.** Longhi's colorful little paintings of the *Sagredo* and *Michiel* families are also worthy of note. Finally, see the portrait of Procurator **Giovanni Querini,** by Tiepolo, and of *Francesco Querini* by Palma the Elder.

Before making your way back to the *Campo SS. Giovanni e Paolo* by way of the *Calle Lunga*, go along to where the *Calle Paradiso* begins in the northwest corner of the *Campo S. Maria Formosa* to see a graceful Gothic arch decorated with a bas-relief of the *Mater Misericordiae*. Note the overhanging beams supporting the upper stories above the pedestrian way.

▬ *AROUND SS. GIOVANNI E PAOLO*

There are four points of interest in or near the *Campo SS. Giovanni e Paolo*: the church of that name, which is a sister church of the *Frari* on the other side of the Grand Canal; the *Scuola di S. Marco*; the equestrian statue of the *condottiere Colleoni*, and the church of *S. Maria dei Miracoli.*

SS. Giovanni e Paolo★★

Map III B-C-6 (Line 5: Fondamente Nuove). *Open 7 am – 12.30 pm and 3.30 – 7.30 pm.*

Zanipolo, as the Venetians fondly call it, is the largest Gothic church in Venice after the *Frari*. This is a fine example of the religious Gothic style which developed here during the 14th and 15th centuries (with some Lombard features) but it also has its own characteristics. The reddish brick building was started, the apse first, during the middle of the 14th century and completed around 1430 but the facade, intended to be very grand, was never, in fact, finished. Zanipolo was, second only to S. Marco, the official church where solemn ceremonies were held and where Doges and other notables are buried. It was built in the shape of a Latin cross with three naves and a transept; ten solid pillars support the ogival vaults. The openwork polygonal apse allows the light to flood into this enormous interior. The United Kingdom plans to restore the stained-glass windows through the *Venice in Peril Fund.*

This is the Venetian Pantheon where famous statesmen and warriors have their last resting place: the tomb of *Doge A. Vendramin* has statues by members of the Lombardo family and is one of the most handsome of its period. Other tombs are those of the Doges *Marco Corner* (by N. Pisano, 14th century), *Morosini* (15th century) and *Loredan* (by Grafiglia, 1572), as well as *Pasquale Malipiero* (by the Lombardos), *M. Steno* and *T. Mocenigo* (by Lamberti and G. di Martino), *N. Marcello* (by P. Lombardo) and *G. Mocenigo* (by T. Lombardo).

As is the case with every church in Venice, this church is also an art gallery.

Along the side-aisle on the right, *The Polyptych of St Vincent Ferrier* (1465) shows the Spanish Dominican between St Christopher and St Sebastian. It is an early work by Giovanni Bellini in which the soft harmonies of the colors are already apparent; in the Chapel of St Dominic, a monumental 18th-century work, the *Apotheosis of St Dominic* (1727) by Piazzetta, is a perfect example of the use of foreshortening and of pyramidal composition – a method at which Tiepolo was to excel. On the ceiling of the Rosary Chapel, which was restored in 1932 after a fire, there are several paintings by Veronese, including a splendid *Adoration of the Shepherds.*

Other works which deserve mention are A. Vivarini's *Christ Carrying His Cross* and Cima da Conegliano's *Crowning of the Virgin*, as well as paintings on Dominican themes by Bassano and Palma the Younger (side-aisle left).

In the *Campo* itself, the most spacious after St Mark's Square, stands one of the finest equestrian statues to be found anywhere, the **Monument to Bartolomeo Colleoni,** a great military leader. This masterpiece of the Renaissance (1488) was cast from a design by Andrea Verrocchio, the great Florentine sculptor who died before it was finished. It was completed by the Venetian Alessandro Leopardi, who also designed the monumental pedestal. It has been recently restored by the *Italia Nostra Fund.*

The **Scuola Grande di S. Marco** is a handsome Renaissance edifice, built by the Lombardos, Antonio Rizzo and Mauro Codussi. It houses part of the hospital and has a particularly handsome marble facade. There are four amazing *trompe-l'œil* compositions by Tullio Lombardo. On the tympanum: *St Mark and Members of the Confraternity.*

The *Rio dei Mendicanti* (the river of beggars), along the side of the hospital, is well known because it is an important north-south waterway. This makes it a highly typical feature of Venice, and both Guardi and Canaletto included it in their paintings. It leads to the *Fondamenta Nuove* where you can find boats for S. Michele, Murano or other islands of the lagoon (lines 5 and 12).

Taking the *Calle Gallina*, you can pay a visit to *S. Maria dei Miracoli* before retracing your steps and continuing on your way.

S. Maria dei Miracoli★★

Map III B-5 (Lines 5: Fondamenta Nuova or 1, 2, or 4: Rialto). *Open 9 am – 12 noon and 3 – 6 pm during the season; open 3 – 4 pm during the off-season. Closed in the afternoon on Sundays and holidays.*

This masterpiece of Renaissance religious architecture was built between 1481 and 1489 by the Lombardos. Decorated with marquetry-like stonework, it gives the impression of a jewel box made of precious wood.

The interior, enhanced by carefully-chosen plaques of cipolin, is no less startling: the wooden vaulted ceiling of the nave consists of 50 compartments, each bearing a portrait of a saint or prophet painted by P. Penacchi (1528); the chancel, unusually raised, is surmounted by a dome.

Above the altar in the apse, you will find Nicolò di Pietro's *Virgin and Child*, a venerated painting which is connected with the beginnings of this church.

▬ *FROM SS. GIOVANNI E PAOLO TO THE GIARDINI PUBBLICI*

From the *Campo SS. Giovanni e Paolo*, follow the *Calle Barbaria delle Tolle* where Casanova lived before going into final exile, then go along the *Rio di S. Lorenzo* and the *Rio di Greci*. Behind the church of S. Zaccaria (*see p. 129*) you will find **S. Giorgio dei Greci,** a little late-Renaissance church. Next to it, the *Instituto Ellenico di Studi Bizantini* has a small **icon museum** containing mostly Veneto-Cretan items. Map III C-4 (Lines 1, 2, 4, 5 or 8: S. Zaccaria or 1: Arsenale). *Open 9 am – 12.30 pm and 3.30 – 6 pm; 9 am – 12 noon on Sundays and holidays. Closed Tuesdays.*

Across the *Rio della Pietà* you will find one of the city's leading artistic buildings, the *Scuola di S. Giorgio degli Schiavoni*.

Scuola di S. Giorgio degli Schiavoni★

Map II C-4 (Lines 1, 2, 4, or 5 or 8: S. Zaccaria or 1: Arsenale). *Open 10 am – 12.30 pm and 3.30 – 6 pm; 10.30 am – 12.30 pm on Sundays and holidays. Closed Mondays. Tel. 52-28-828.*

It was founded by the Confraternity of the Schiavoni, Dalmatians who, having settled in Venice, were attempting to assist each other by collecting dowries for their daughters, helping the poor and sick, and praying for the dead. The building is noteworthy for its Carpaccio paintings. The ground floor was remodeled in the 17th century when the paintings, intended originally for the first floor, were placed in it. The finest are, without doubt, **St George Killing the Dragon,** a masterly composition in which the harmony of the colors does

The onion-shaped domes of San Marco dominate a sea of roofs.

nothing to lessen the general impression of violence; *The Triumph of St George*; **St Matthew Leading the Lion to the Monastery,** a canvas marked by imagination and movement; *The Death of St Jerome* and **The Vision of St Augustine** – the latter, a remarkable composition famous for the little dog in it, is important for being the first known rendition of a Renaissance humanist's study.

On the first floor, there is a fine coffered ceiling and paintings from the Palma the Younger school.

On the Riva degli Schiavoni, by the Rio dei Greci, stands the modest **Pietà** church (Map II C-4, Lines 1, 2, 4, 5 or 8: S. Zaccaria), dedicated to the Visitation. The facade is almost Classical and there is a fine ceiling by Tiepolo, *The Crowning of* *the Virgin.* The church was renowned in the 18th century for music lessons given by Vivaldi to the young boarders of the convent.

The Church of **S. Giovanni in Bragora** (Map II C-4), a short distance from the quay, was founded in the 8th century and rebuilt in the 15th century. It has several works by A. Vivarini, including a *Resurrection*, a splendid *Baptism of Christ* by Cima da Conegliano and a *Last Supper* by Paris Bordone. Vivaldi was baptized here.

A short distance away stands the main entrance to the **Arsenale** (1460). (Map II C-5, Line 1: Arsenale; Line 5 goes past it) with its allegorical statues and four lions brought back from one of the campaigns of the Most Serene Republic. The public is not admitted, as the Arsenale retains its military function, but you can still cast a glance at a building which was Europe's first modern factory and the foundation of Venice's naval power.

Then, by going along the *Rio dell 'Arsenale*, you come to the naval museum, on the *Riva S. Biagio.*

Museo Storico Navale

Map II D-5 (Line 1: Arsenale). *Open 9 am – 1 pm; 12 noon on Saturdays. Closed Sundays and holidays. Tel. 70-02-76.*

The museum is not devoted solely to the history of Venice's navy, but ranges over the whole of Italy's naval history. It also possesses a quite incredible collection of Far Eastern junks. You will find here models of Venetian naval craft, including the famous *Bucintoro*, the Doge's ceremonial barge, and an interesting collection of compasses.

You can bring your itinerary to a close by going along the quays as far as the **Giardini Pubblici** (Map II D-E-5-6, Line 1: Giardini-Esposizione) laid out by order of Napoleon, where you will find the exhibition halls of the famous International Bienniale of Modern Art.

THE VENETIAN LAGOON
AND ITS ENVIRONS

If you can spare a few days, you will be tempted to go outside the limits of old Venice to visit the surrounding area, a temptation which is not easy to resist because it means going by boat through very attractive scenery.

Some of the islands are just a few minutes away from St Mark's Square: S. Giorgio Maggiore and La Giudecca, for instance. Others require a half-day visit, like Murano, the Lido, Burano and Torcello. If you want to go to the end of the lagoon, to Chiòggia, you will probably need a full day.

THE LAGOON

The beauty of the Venetian Lagoon captivates every visitor – whether it is the beauty of nature, or the beauty created by the builders of churches and palaces. On a smaller scale, the intricate lace and glassware produced by hard-working local people is also very attractive.

If you feel more attracted by landscapes and the pleasures of the seaside, and less by the world of glassblowers, lacemakers and ancient sanctuaries, we advise you to visit the southern part of the lagoon rather than the north. The one does not exclude the other, of course, but it must be said that the slow decline of Venice has left scars on the famous islands of *Murano*, *Burano* and even *Torcello* that are undeniably more visible than in the city itself. The Lido, however, has benefited from new buildings and gardens which, although not always beautiful, are well-kept and glow with the particular charm of modern "kitsch" – one example is the great complex of the Royal Excelsior. Fishing villages like *Malamocco, S. Pietro in Volta, Pellestrina* and the port of *Chiòggia* offer a colorful and lively spectacle of men and their boats, and of the ever-changing sea and the ageless lagoon.

▬ S. GIORGIO MAGGIORE AND LA GIUDECCA

The islands of S. Giorgio Maggiore and La Giudecca are only a short distance away from St Mark's Square and *Dorsoduro*. They could easily be included in the previous itineraries, especially C and F. The easiest way to get there is to take a motorboat (Line 5) from the *Zattere* or, if you are coming from the opposite direction, leave from *S. Zaccaria* on the *Riva degli Schiavoni*.

S. Giorgio Maggiore★★

This island, opposite the Palace of the Doges, was frequented by sailors long before the *Rialto*.

Called Cypress Island until the 9th century, when a church was built there in honor of St George, it owes its importance to a Benedictine monastery erected in the 10th century: this became a center of culture, the influence of which lasted until the Napoleonic period when it was closed down and used for military purposes (1806). Its art treasures and the contents of its *library* were scattered but they have been traced and gradually brought back since 1950 when the *Foundation Giorgio Cini* purchased the buildings. They have been painstakingly restored and the island has regained its original vocation as a center of learning and professional training. The Foundation finances a Merchant Navy School which has several ships at its disposal and is intended to train the orphaned children of seamen and fishermen. It also funds a School of Arts and Trades specializing in printing and mechanical trades as well as an International Center of Art and Culture which sponsors publications, organizes congresses, exhibitions and, on occasion, musical and dramatic performances in an open-air theater. The church, cloisters and refectory were begun in 1556 from plans by Andrea Palladio, and completed 50 years later by Vincenzo Scamozzi. Baldassare Longhena then added the magnificent library and the splendid grand staircase (1671).

The **church of S. Giorgio Maggiore,** Map II D-4 (Line 5: S. Giorgio). *Open 9 am – 12.30 pm and 2 – 8.30 pm.* With its Renaissance facade, resplendent above a wide square which comes down to the edge of the lagoon, the church forms an essential feature of the superb vista which can be admired from the *Molo* or the *Piazzetta*. In turn, it provides an incomparable view of the City of the Doges.

As soon as you enter, you will be struck by the feeling of power and grandeur created by the balance and simplicity of the interior. It also contains a number of masterpieces of Venetian art. At the first altar on the right aisle, Bassano's last work, *The Nativity*, offers an extraordinary nocturnal vision of the scene; dazzling light radiates from the Infant Jesus and shines on the faces of the shepherds. On the chancel wall, to the right, Tintoretto's **Last Supper** is remarkable for the extraordinary effect obtained by the use of color, zones of shadows contrasting strongly with the brightness of the lamp shedding its light over the scene. His *Manna in the Desert* on the opposite wall is a luminous and complex country scene in which the characters evoke rural life. The walnut *choir stalls* are carved with scenes from the life of St Benedict by the

The church of Murano – this island is famed for its glassworks, established centuries ago and influenced by Roman and Eastern traditions.

Flemish artist, Van der Brulle. To the right of the choir, a door opens onto a corridor leading to a chapel where you may see yet another Tintoretto, *The Deposition of Christ*, above the altar. A spiral staircase takes you to the Conclave Room where Pope Pius VII was proclaimed Pope during the Napoleonic period; it is unfortunately now closed to visitors.

We urge you to go to the top of the *campanile (by elevator, access through the left transept, 9 am – 12.15 pm and 2.30 – 7.30 pm. Tel. 52-89-900)* which provides a view no less splendid than does its *S. Marco* counterpart. This campanile has the advantage of being less crowded. If the weather is clear, the panorama over city and lagoon is breathtaking.

La Giudecca

The island of La Giudecca was the old Jewish quarter of Venice. It is now a suburb with gardens, apartment blocks and factories. Its calm atmosphere, unusual for Venice, makes a visit well worthwhile. Of special note are its three churches with their white facades facing the quays of *Dorsoduro* districts: **Zitelle** (Map II E-3; Line 5: Ostello), **S. Eufemia** (Map II E-2; Line 5: S. Eufemia) and, above all, the Redentore*.

Il Redentore* (Church of the Redeemer, Map II E-3; Line 5: Redentore. *Open 8 am – 12 noon and 3.30 – 7 pm*), was built by Palladio and Da Ponte after the 1576 plague. It has a pure classical facade and a dome over a single nave, where twinned pillars alternate with altars over which hang paintings by Francesco Bassano, Palma the Younger and pupils of Tintoretto. You can see in the sacristy a *Virgin Adoring the Sleeping Child* by A. Vivarini (1489), a *Baptism of Christ* of the Veronese school, and works by Bassano, Palma the Younger, F. Bissolo, and F. Bastiani. During the *Festa del Redentore* (3rd weekend in July), one of the most colorful festivals in Venice, the island of Giudecca is linked to the *Zattere* by a pontoon bridge.

▬ THE NORTH OF THE LAGOON

Two lines of motorboats ply to the northern islands: Line 5 for S. Michele and Murano which are only a few minutes away from the *Fondamenta Nuove*; Line 12 for Murano, Torcello and Burano, roughly an hour away from the *Fondamenta Nuove*. If you decide to see all four islands you should allow a full day.

S. Michele

Map II A-4 (Line 5: S. Michele).

Enclosed within walls of pink brick and covered with cypresses, the island of S. Michele is Venice's cemetery, as romantic as anyone could wish for and one of the very few in the world where funeral processions go by sea. Stravinsky and Diaghilev are buried here.

The church of *S. Michele* is one of the oldest Renaissance-style religious buildings in Venice (built by Codussi from 1469 to 1478). Beside it stands the *Emiliani Chapel*, a graceful structure by G. Bergamasco (1530).

Murano★

Map II A-B-5-6 (Line 5 or 12: Colonna or Faro).

This island is famed for the glassware it has been producing since 1290 when the Most Serene Republic decided to move out the glass workers to save the city from the possible danger of fire caused by the furnaces. In the 15th century, it was also the center of the Vivarini School of painting and consequently played an important role in the introduction of the Renaissance to Venice. It had 30,000 inhabitants in the 16th century, but has only 7000 today and many once-flourishing workshops have been abandoned.

"Strict laws were decreed to safeguard the secrets of the master glassmakers. Murano has always maintained its superiority in the manufacture of light, shining blown glass of a particularly harmonious design. Nothing is more impressive than watching one of these objects being created with a confident skill that has been transmitted from father to son, and seeing a formless, incandescent mass take on the shape of a fragile *fiala* (bottle), a flower or a delicately colored dish." (R. Pallucchini). You will, because that is Murano's special attraction, be able to visit the glassmakers' workshops along the right bank of the canal which ends at the *Colonna* landing stage (Fondamenta dei Vitrai). A little farther off, on the left, the **Church of S. Pietro Martire,** founded in the 14th century and reconstructed in 1511, has paintings by Veronese,

Tintoretto and a fine *Madonna* by Giovanni Bellini. Across the bridge, the *Fondamenta Marco Giustinian* leads to the glassware museum.

The **Museo d'Arte Vetraria,** Map II A-6 (*Open 10 am – 4 pm; 9.30 am – 12.30 pm Sundays and holidays. Closed Wednesdays. Tel. 73-95-86*). This museum is situated in the handsome Palazzo Giustinian (17th century). It contains a valuable collection of some 4000 items spanning the whole history of glassmaking from antiquity to the present day. A short distance away, you will find the **Basilica of SS. Maria e Donato,** with its separate campanile; the basilica was founded in the 7th century and rebuilt in brick in Ravenna Byzantine style in the 12th century. Note particularly the mosaic floor (1140) depicting fantastic animals, peacocks and eagles, and, on the apse vault, the *mosaic of the Virgin Madre di Dio* on a gold background, a Byzantine work of the 13th century. When you first go in, walk towards the apse with its two unusual superimposed galleries showing off the contrast between the brickwork and the white Istrian stone columns and balustrades. Important works include: *The Death of the Virgin* in the left side-aisle, a late 14th-century polyptych in the style of L. Veneziano; above the baptistery entrance, a *Virgin and Child* by L. Bastiani (1484); behind, *St Donato*, a polychrome relief panel of 1310 attributed to Paolo Veneziano.

Torcello ★★

Map I (Line 12: Torcello). If you want to have lunch at the *Locanda Cipriani*, take the midday *Harry's Bar* motorboat from the *S. Marco* landing stage.

Once a wealthy city of 20,000 inhabitants, a bishop's see and an independent municipality, Torcello now consists of a handful of houses and some market gardens growing fruit and vegetables which are greatly prized by the people of Venice. It was overshadowed by the *Rialto* and forsaken by its inhabitants as too unhealthy but it has two buildings which are among the most interesting in Venice.

The **Church of S. Fosca,★** built in the 11th century, is octagonal in shape and surrounded on five sides by a portico linking it to the cathedral.

The triple nave interior features pillars of Greek marble. The mosaic floor and reliefs date from the 11th century, and there are 15th-century paintings.

The **Cathedral of S. Maria Assunta★** (*Open daily 10 am – 12.30 pm and 2 – 6.30 pm. Tel. 73-00-84*) was much admired by Hemingway, its sober architecture is quite exceptional. Founded in the 7th century and rebuilt in the 11th, it is undeniably one of the finest religious edifices in Veneto-Byzantine style anywhere in the Adriatic.

The Torcello International Committee has financed a program to clear the algae developing on the stones; the crypt, affected by stagnant water, has to be restored; the western facade has been covered with a waterproof resin that will still enable the walls to breathe. This sober frontage has a narthex and the portico links it to the nearby church of *S. Fosca*.

The front interior wall is decorated with an amazing mosaic in which anonymous Veneto-Byzantine artists of the 12th and 13th centuries, drawing their inspiration from Oriental proto- types interpreted in a Romanesque way, depicted the *Apotheosis of Christ* and the *Last Judgement*. The mosaic is divided into six sections showing such episodes as *Christ's Descent into Limbo, the Archangel Michael Weighing Souls While the Devil Awaits his Share, The Resurrection of the Dead,* with other symbols such as the *Hetimasia,* and *Hell* with the damned being punished according to their sins. The mosaicists of S. Marco are restoring the Torcello mosaics and affixing them back on the wall. Also see the *Virgin and Apostles* (12th-13th centuries) in the apse.

In front of the cathedral, the **Museo dell'Estuario** has collections of archaeological items, sculpture and some works of art. *Open 10 am – 12.30 pm and 2 – 5.30 pm. Closed Mondays. Tel. 73-07-61.*

Burano

Map I (Line 12: Burano).

The island of Burano is the most picturesque of the northern lagoon islands. Here, the men fish and women make lace, and the houses are painted in bright, almost fluorescent, colors, especially reds and blues.

Densely populated (6000 inhabitants) in a relatively small area, it is almost entirely built along two canals lined with quays up from which wind narrow *calli* reached through porticos here and there between the houses. It is a colorful Mediterranean world that seems like a foretaste of the Greek islands. The lacemakers work in front of their houses and sell their wares from stands set up near the landing stage. The lace industry began in the 16th century at the suggestion of the Dogaressa Duodo.

There is a lacemakers' school in the *Palazzo del Podestà*, a Gothic structure. The church of *S. Martino* (16th century) has a remarkable leaning *campanile*.

From Burano you can take a motorboat to visit **S. Francisco del Deserto,** an unusual little island, 20 minutes away, which is more insular than all the others. It is believed St Francis of Assisi landed there in 1220. The monastery is surrounded by a line of cypresses which accentuates the sense of isolation (*Open 9 am – 11 am and 3 – 5.30 pm. A donation is cus- tomary. Tel. 52-86-863*).

THE SOUTH OF THE LAGOON

From the Lido to Chiòggia, the lagoon is protected from the Adriatic Sea by a succession of offshore sand bars (*lidi* in Italian) which have become seaside resorts. We recommend, for a visit to the south of the lagoon (excluding S. Lazzaro degli Armeni), taking a motorboat (1, 2 or 4) from Venice to the *Lido*, then the bus (11) from the *Lido* to *Pellestrina*, crossing the *Malamocco* gap to the ferry, and then taking the *motobatello* from *Pellestrina* to *Chiòggia*. To come back, we suggest you take the *motonave* 25 from *Chiòggia* to *Pellestrina, S. Pietro in Volta* and Venice, a journey of 1 hr. 40 min. A full day is required for such a trip.

The island of Burano in the center of the Lagoon: modest houses painted in vivid colors with fishing boats moored alongside the quay.

S. Lazzaro degli Armeni

Map I (Line 20 from S. Zaccaria on Riva degli Schiavoni; depart at 3 pm, return from S. Lazzaro at 5 pm).

This island, close to the Lido, is of considerable historical and documentary importance. It was a former lepers' hospital, given in 1717 by the Most Serene Republic to Father Mechitar and a group of Armenians driven out by the Turks. A real Armenian colony, it became a great center of Armenian religion, culture and philosophy.

A fire ravaged the convent in 1976; it spared the superb air-conditioned library with its ancient Armenian manuscripts and books but the modern printing press was completely destroyed. There is a small museum which contains works by Palma the Younger and Tiepolo.

The Lido

Map I and the map on p. 146 (Lines 1, 2, or 4 from Piazzale Roma or the Rialto, 6 or 21 from the Riva degli Schiavoni, or with your car, ferry 17 from Piazzale Roma).

Byron and Shelley both liked to ride on the damp sand from one end of this narrow 7 mile/12 km tongue of land to the other. Since those days, an elegant seaside resort has grown up along the shore, a mere quarter of an hour from Venice's historic center.

The beautiful stretch of fine sand, the hotels, the *casino* (one of only four allowed in Italy), the sports facilities (golf, tennis, pigeon shooting, etc.) all contribute to its fame as an international vacationers' paradise.

Boats land at the *Piazzale S. M. Elisabetta* in front of the church of the same name. Opposite the landing stage, the *Gran Viale S. M. Elisabetta* stretches out towards the *Piazzale Bucintoro* which ends in a terrace overlooking the beach. From there, to the right, the great boulevard, the *Lungomare Marconi*, leads to the casino and the film center.

The beach has several rows of bathing huts; try, at any price, to get one in the front row as the others rapidly become stifling (if you are not successful, it might be wiser to change in your hotel or your car).

There is one building that has been much talked about since its partial collapse a few years ago: **Fort Sant 'Andrea,** a masterpiece of Venetian military architecture by the great *Sanmicheli* (16th century). Also note the *murazzi*, as you walk along the beach towards Alberoni. These are strange-looking structures of Istrian stone and prestressed concrete tetrapods, the function of which is to protect the shore and the lagoon from the onslaughts of the sea.

On your way from the *Lido* to *Chiòggia* you will come to the village of **Malamocco,** one of the earliest settlements of the *Veneti.* Victim of the ceaseless tides, it has lost all trace of those distant origins. Now it is an orderly fishing village on the shore of the lagoon from where you can admire the city of Venice silhouetted against the most beautiful sunsets.

Alberoni, at the end of this coastal strip, offers vacationers its golf course, a fine, popular beach with a quieter beach and sand dunes further on.

The **Pellestrina coast** follows on from the Lido beyond the *Malamocco* channel. It has the appearance of a long sea-wall sheltering a line of villages clustered on the lagoon side with their backs to the sea. It is a 6 mile/10 km trip without much of a sea-view.

The villages of **S. Pietro in Volta** and **Pellestrina** are quite charming little spots, and each has restaurants offering excellent fish menus. If you like a flavor of sea-life, don't miss this trip.

Chiòggia∗

Finally, you get to a typically original, small town, a totally Mediterranean atmosphere with fish stalls set up between a sunlit basin and shady arcades under the houses along the quays. This mini-Venice, built on an isthmus, is linked to the mainland by two bridges.

The *Corso del Popolo* begins in front of the landing stage and runs through the town. As you walk along it you see, in turn, the church of *S. Andrea* with its Romanesque tower, the market, the Communal Palace and the church of *S. Giacomo* (18th-century interior). On the right, the church of *S. Martino*

(1392) with its octagonal tower. The **Duomo** still has its 14th-century campanile from which there is a splendid view. Inside the church, there are paintings by Tiepolo and Piazzetta. In the **church of S. Domenico,** above the second altar to the right, you will find the last work of Vittore Carpaccio: *St Paul* (1520).

To get back to Venice, you take either *motonave* 25, as suggested above, or the bus that will bring you to the *Piazzale Roma* by the overland route in less than an hour: the countryside won't be anything special but it will save you time. In fact, the latter form of transport used both ways would allow you to visit Chiòggia in a mere half-day although, if you are visiting it at your leisure, it is best to leave a full day for the trip.

THE RIVIERA DEL BRENTA

A daily cruise is available from Venice to Padua by the Brenta canal. This is a journey of 19 miles/31 km in a specially equipped *vaporetto*, called *Il Burchiello* (with lunch at Oriago). Alternatively, you can go in the launch, *La Smeralda* (with lunch at Mira); hostess, bar and all the usual conveniences are available in both vessels. These facilities are available from April 15 to September 30 during the season.

Book at the C.I.T., under the arcades, southern side of St Mark's Square (*tel. 52-85-480*) or at any travel agent. Departures from Venice on Tuesdays, Thursdays, Fridays, Saturdays and Sundays; from Padua on Wednesdays, Thursdays, Fridays, Saturdays and Sundays. The return journey is by bus. The trip takes a whole day because of the speed limit imposed on boats (3 mph/5 km/h) and the many locks to be negotiated. We recommend the cruise if you are not too pressed for time; otherwise we would suggest a half-day trip by road. There are only four or five stops, depending on which boat you select.

Reviving interest in the Riviera del Brenta was an excellent idea; the drawback is the atmospheric pollution caused by the factories of Marghera and the all-too-visible pollution of the water and banks of the canal.

The trip enables you to admire (sometimes from a little too low down) dozens of beautiful villas built there by Venetian noblemen. For centuries, the banks of the Brenta were popular with the aristocracy of Venice and, here, evening fêtes with garden illuminations, concerts and balls were given; orchestras, hidden in the shrubbery, played music by Pergolesi, Cimarosa and Vivaldi. The ancestor of today's *vaporetto* was an 18th-century rowing barge linking Padua and Venice, hauled along the canal by a horse (you will be shown the post-houses where the horses were changed), ferrying lords and their ladies, merchants, artists and actors, adventur-

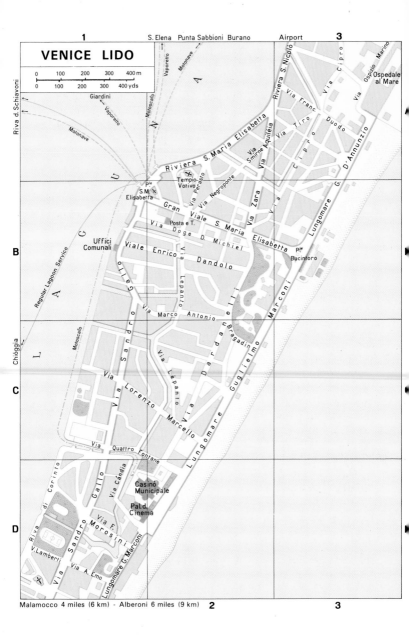

VENICE LIDO

S. Elena Punta Sabbioni Burano   Airport

Riva d.Schiavoni

Giardini

0   100   200   300   400 m
0   100   200   300   400 yds

Vaporetto
Motonave
Vaporetto
Motoscafo
Motonave
Regular Lagoon Service
Chióggia
Motoscafo

Riviera S. Maria Elisabetta
Riviera S. Nicolò
Via Franc
Via Cipro
Via Tiro
Via C i p r o
Via Franc
Duodo
G. D'Annunzio
Ospizio Marino
Ospedale al Mare

Tempio Votivo
Pl⁰ S.M. Elisabetta
Gran Viale S. Maria Elisabetta
Via Perasto
Via Negroponte
Via Smirne
Via Aquiléia
Via Zara

Uffici Comunali
Posta e T.
Via Doge D. Michiel
Viale Enrico Dandolo
Via Lepanto
Pl⁰ Bucintoro
Lungomare G.

B

Gallo
Via Corpus
Via Marco Antonio Bragadin
Via Sandro
Via Guglielmo Marconi

C

Via Lorenzo Marcello
Via Lepanto Marcello
Lungomare G. Marconi
Quattro Fontane
Via

Riva di Corinto
Via Gallo
Via Candia
Via F. Morosini
Via Sandro
V. Lamberti
Via A. Emo
Lungomare G. Marconi
Casinò Municipale
Pal.d. Cinema

D

Malamocco 4 miles (6 km) - Alberoni 6 miles (9 km) **2**   **3**

ers and women of easy virtue. It was a famous boat, extolled by Casanova and Goldoni, painted by Canaletto, mentioned by Byron, Goethe and Montaigne.

As you go through the locks and swing-bridges you will be able to see·not only the villas, palaces and little casinos, but also industrial complexes and some rather seedy-looking dwellings. You will nevertheless have the opportunity to stop at two quite remarkable villas.

The Villa Foscari★ in Oriago is an admirable building by

Andrea Palladio. The facade overlooking an English-style garden (the first thing you see), is a little austere but, as you walk on, with the picturesque rustic stables to your left, you quickly come upon the facade with a Greek portico on the canal side. To be frank, the real value of this building is its perfectly proportioned interior, each room with polychrome pastel frescoes of differing motifs, and with a different dominant color. Note the *trompe-l'œil* effect of medallions, pillars and entablatures around the doors). This villa is often referred to as "La Malcontenta" because it was once the residence in exile of the unfaithful wife of a nobleman of the *Foscari* family who was highly dissatisfied with her lot.

The Pisani Villa in Strà is the size of a castle. It is the most imposing of all the Brenta villas built for the Doges of the Pisani family. It has 200 reception rooms decorated by the greatest artists of the 18th century. The ballroom ceiling is decorated with a fresco by Tiepolo, an extraordinary *Apotheosis of the Pisani Family* (1762).

You will no doubt be told that, in addition to famous members of the House of Austria and *King Gustav III* of Sweden, the house has numbered among its residents *Napoleon I* who bought it in 1807. You should know that *Hitler* and *Mussolini* held their first meeting here in 1934, a setting appropriate to the scale of their insane dreams.

In the park you will find the **stables,** an ice house and the famous 18th-century **maze** described by *D'Annunzio* in his novel *Il Fuoco.*

When driving down this way, you should stop at Mira to visit the **Villa Widmann** (1719), with its many frescoes, where *Cardinal Rezzonico,* later *Pope Clement XIII,* and *Carlo Goldoni* were guests; the **Villa Contarini** and the **Palazzo Contarini** where Byron composed the fourth canto of *Childe Harold* (1817-19), and the **Villa Lazara Pisani,** called "La Barbariga" (in Strà) the facade of which is decorated with festoons of climbing plants.

THE VENETIAN VILLAS AROUND VICENZA

The trip is available by coach or train (1 hour): inquire at any travel agency. If you are attracted by Palladian villas, we advise you to visit these Venetian country homes, or at least the two most famous ones: the Villa Valmarana and the "Rotonda" featured in Losey's lavish film of *Don Giovanni.*

The Villa Valmarana

Open March 15 to November 4, Monday to Saturday 3.30 – 6.30 pm, Sundays and holidays 10 am – 12 noon. Closed Sundays, holidays and November 5 to March 14.

Known as the *Villa ai Nani* (the dwarfs' villa) it comprises several buildings: the master's house, guest house, stables and outbuildings.

It was built by Antonio Muttoni in the Venetian style, at the end of the 17th century (from 1669). Don't miss the great drawing-room in the master's house which extends the full length of the building. It has a remarkable fresco of *The Sacrifice of Iphigenia*; on the ground floor, you will find frescoes depicting scenes from *Orlando Furioso* and the *Iliad*. All these soft-hued paintings are by Giambattista Tiepolo, assisted at times by his son Giandomenico who also painted the charming frescoes of daily life and the Chinese motifs in the guest house.

La Rotonda

Open daily 10 am – 12 noon and 4 – 6 pm. Closed in the afternoons during holidays.

This house Palladio's most famous villa, was started in 1550 and completed by Scamozzi after the great architect's death. Four replicas exist in England. A typical example of the dramatic use of space, this villa, with the rotunda from which it gets its name, oriented towards the four points of the compass, is a real house of magic in which Palladio has brought the universe down to human scale.

Apart from the perfect geometry and balanced simplicity of this beautiful building, notice how a sense of cool freshness is created by the large number of apertures. The interior decoration (late 16th-early 17th century), is the work of Rubini and Maganza, completed in the early years of the 18th century by Dorigny. Outside, there are statues by Rubini (1571) and reliefs by Albanese (*c.* 1600).

If you have time to spare in the area around Vicenza, try to visit the following places:
– north of Vicenza: the **Castello Porto Colleoni** (1476) in Thiene (12 miles/20 km from Vicenza), and the **Villa Godi-Malinverni** (the first creation of Palladio in 1540) at Lonedo di Lugo (18½ miles/30 km)
– south of Vicenza: the **Villa Pojana** at Pojana Maggiore (25 miles/40.5 km). A unique work by *Palladio* (1566), with statues by G. Albanese (1658), frescoes by B. India and A. Canera, and stuccoes by Ridolfi.

BIBLIOGRAPHY

Venice: Descriptions, General

Bull, George: *Venice, the Most Triumphant City* (St Martin's, New York, 1982)

Lauritzen, P., and A. Zielke: *Palaces of Venice* (Viking, New York, 1978)

Morris, Jan: *A Venice Bestiary* (Thames & Hudson, London, 1982)

Roiter, Fulvio: *Venice* (Viking, New York, 1979)

Ruskin, John: *The Stones of Venice* (first published 1853) (Little, Boston, 1981)

Art, History, Literature

Finlay, Robert: *Politics in Renaissance Venice* (Rutgers University, Brunswick, NJ, 1980)

Lauritzen, Peter: *Venice, a Thousand Years of Culture and Civilization* (Atheneum, New York, 1978)

Levey, M.: *Painting in Eighteenth-Century Venice* (University of London, 1959)

Logan, Oliver: *Culture and Society in Venice 1470-1790* (Batsford, London, 1972)

McAndrew, John: *Venetian Architecture of the Early Renaissance* (M.I.T., Cambridge, MA, 1980)

McNeill, William H.: *Venice, the Hinge of Europe 1081-1797* (University of Chicago, 1974)

Norwich, John J.: *A History of Venice* (Knopf, New York, 1982)

Riggs, Arthur S.: *Titian the Magnificent and the Venice of his Day* (Bobbs, New York, 1946)

Schultz, J.: *Venetian Painted Ceilings of the Renaissance* (University of California, Berkeley, 1968)

Wowthorne, S.T.: *Venetian Opera in the Seventeenth Century* (Oxford University Press, 1954)

— USEFUL VOCABULARY

Common words and phrases

Yes	*Si*
No	*No*
Sir	*Signore*
Madam	*Signora*
Miss	*Signorina*
Good morning/Hello	*Buongiorno*
Hello (answering tel.)	*Pronto*
Good evening	*Buonasera*
Good night	*Buona notte*
Good bye	*Arrivederci*
I am sorry	*Mi scusi*
Please	*Per favore*
Thank you	*Grazie*
Please, do not mention it	*Prego*
Why?	*Perché?*
What?	*Che cosa?*
Where?	*Dov'è?*
Who?	*Chi?*
When?	*Quando?*
Far	*Lontano*
Near	*Vicino*
More	*Ancora*
Can you tell me?	*Può dirmi?*
Do you have?	*Ha?*
I do not understand	*Non capisco*
Speak slowly	*Parli lentamente*
A lot, very	*Molto*
Few, a little	*Poco*
Too much	*Troppo*
Enough	*Abbastanza*
All, everything	*Tutto*
Nothing	*Niente*
How much?	*Quanto costa?*
It is too expensive	*E' troppo caro*

Numbers

One	*Uno*
Two	*Due*
Three	*Tre*
Four	*Quattro*
Five	*Cinque*
Six	*Sei*
Seven	*Sette*
Eight	*Otto*
Nine	*Nove*
Ten	*Dieci*
Eleven	*Undici*
Twelve	*Dodici*
Thirteen	*Tredici*
Fourteen	*Quattordici*
Fifteen	*Quindici*
Sixteen	*Sedici*
Seventeen	*Diciassette*
Eighteen	*Diciotto*
Nineteen	*Diciannove*
Twenty	*Venti*
Twenty-one	*Ventuno*
Twenty-two	*Ventidue*
Thirty	*Trenta*
Forty	*Quaranta*

Fifty	*Cinquanta*
Sixty	*Sessanta*
Seventy	*Settanta*
Eighty	*Ottanta*
Ninety	*Novanta*
One hundred	*Cento*
Two hundred	*Duecento*
Three hundred	*Trecento*
One thousand	*Mille*
Two thousand	*Duemila*
Three thousand	*Tremila*
One million	*Un milione*

At the station, at the airport

A ticket to	*Un biglietto per*
At what time does it leave?	*A che ora parte?*
At what time does it arrive?	*A che ora arriva?*
From what platform does the train leave?	*Di quale binario parte il treno?*
To arrive	*Arrivare*
To change	*Cambiare*
Berth	*Cuccetta*
Guard	*Controllore*
To leave	*Partire*
Left luggage office	*Deposito*
Luggage	*Bagagli*
Platform	*Binario*
Porter	*Facchino*
Station	*Stazione*
Stop	*Fermata*
Suitcase	*Valigia*
Taxi	*Tassì* or *taxi*
Taxi rank	*Posteggio di tassì*
Train	*Treno*
Ticket	*Biglietto*
Timetable	*Orario*

Driving

Air	*Gonfiaggio*
Attention danger	*Attenzione pericoloso*
Car	*Macchina*
Car wash	*Lavaggio*
Entrance	*Ingresso*
Exit	*Uscita*
Forbidden	*Vietato*
Grease, lubrication	*Lubrificazione*
No parking	*Divieto di sosta*
Oil	*Olio*
Parking	*Parcheggio*
Pay toll	*Pedaggio*
Petrol, gas	*Benzina*
Right	*A destra*
Left	*A sinistra*
Road under repair	*Lavori in corso*
Slippery surface	*Fondo sdrucciolevole*
Tire	*Pneumatico*

In town

Alley	*Vicolo*
Avenue	*Viale*
Cemetery	*Campo Santo, cimetero*
Church	*Chiesa*

Cloister	*Chiostro*
Courtyard	*Cortile*
Garden	*Giardino, orto*
Market	*Mercato*
Museum	*Museo*
Palace	*Palazzo*
Ruins	*Rovine*
Square	*Piazza, largo*
Square (large)	*Piazzale*
Stairs	*Scala*
Street	*Via*
Walk	*Promenade*

Time

Monday	*Lunedi*
Tuesday	*Martedi*
Wednesday	*Mercoledi*
Thursday	*Giovedi*
Friday	*Venerdi*
Saturday	*Sabato*
Sunday	*Domenica*
Spring	*Primavera*
Summer	*Estate*
Autumn	*Autunno*
Winter	*Inverno*
Today	*Oggi*
Yesterday	*Ieri*
The day before yesterday	*Ieri l'altro*
Tomorrow	*Domani*
The day after tomorrow	*Dopo domani*
In the morning	*La mattina*
In the afternoon	*Nel pomeriggio*
In the evening	*La sera*

At the hotel

Inn, Bed & Breakfast	*Locanda*
Hotel	*Albergo*
Boarding-house	*Una pensione familiare*
I would like a room	*Desidero una camera*
With one bed, with two beds	*A un letto, a due letti*
Room with bath	*Camera con bagno*
On the street	*Sulla strada*
Not on the street	*Interna, sul cortile*
What is the price, including tax and service?	*Qual'è il prezzo, servizio e tasse comprese?*
English breakfast	*Colazione all'inglese*
What time is lunch served?	*A che ora è il pranzo?*
And dinner?	*E la cena?*
Wake me up at ... o'clock	*Mi svegli alle ... ore*
I would like the bill	*Vorrei il conto*

At the restaurant

Apple	*Mela*
Beer	*Birra*
Bread	*Pane*
Butter	*Burro*
Cheese	*Formaggio*
Chicken	*Pollo*
Coffee	*Caffé*
Coffee with cream	*Cappuccino*
Cover charge	*Coperto*
Dessert	*Dolce*

Egg	*Uovo*
Fish	*Pesce*
Fork	*Forchetta*
Fruit	*Frutta*
Fruit juice	*Succo di frutta*
Glass	*Bicchiere*
Grapes	*Uva*
Ham	*Prosciutto*
Hot chocolate	*Cioccolata (in tazza*
Knife	*Coltello*
Lamb	*Agnello, abbachio*
Main course	*Pasto*
Meal	*Pasto*
Menu, list	*Lista*
Mustard	*Mostardo*
Mutton	*Castrato*
Omelette	*Frittata*
Orange	*Arancia*
Pasta	*Pasta*
Pepper	*Pepe*
Plate, dish	*Piatto*
Pork	*Maiale*
Potato	*Patata*
Salad	*Insalata*
Salami	*Salame*
Salt	*Sale*
Simple restaurant	*Trattoria*
Soup	*Zuppa, brodo*
Spoon (teaspoon)	*Cucchiaio (Cucchiaino)*
Starter	*Antipasti*
Steak	*Bistecca*
Sweet	*Dolce*
Sugar	*Zucchero*
Tea	*Tè*
Veal	*Vitello*
Veal chop	*Costata di vitello*
Vegetables	*Verdura*
Waiter	*Cameriere*
Water	*Acqua*
Wine (Red)	*Vino (rosso)*
Wine (white)	*Vino (bianco)*

INDEX

Printed in Singapore by Tien Wah Press
Dépôt légal: 3796-1-1987
ISBN 0-7230-0290-8